TALES OF THE
SUPER RICH

**By Dexter Yager
and
Doug Wead**

Typesetting by Type-O-Graphics
Springfield, Mo. 65806

Dedicated to our parents Leonard and Gertrude Yager and Roy and Rosa Mae Wead for their guidance, love and counseling in the early years of our lives.

Contents

1 Palaces and Pleasure Domes   7
William Astor Buys a Castle

2 Spending Sprees   24
Howard Hughes' Ice Cream Caper

3 Feasts and Fetes   38
Chocolates for Diamond Jim

4 The Last Resort   52
The Vanderbilt's Hot Springs Hideaway

5 Wedding Veils and Vagabonds   64
The Fairy Tale Wedding of Monte Carlo

6 Toy Boats   82
Onassis' Floating Palace

7 Wheels   99
Mrs. Twombly's Violet Rolls-Royce

8 A Generous Heart   107
J. P. Morgan Saves a Bank

9 Hard Work and Risk   133
Vanderbilt's Hundred Dollar Loan

1

Palaces and Pleasure Domes

William Astor Buys a Castle

Sunshine like Croesus' gold glinted off the
deep turquoise waves of the Mediterranean.
White sand reflected the rays, as if the sea were
backlit by some great underwater Tiffany lamp.
Elsewhere along the French Riviera, bikinied
crowds clamored and radios blared raucous
music, but not here on the thumb of the
Cap d'Antibes. This private beach was
undisturbed by outsiders, quiet except for the
lap of the waves, the song of the great white
gulls dipping in joyous minuet, and the happy
laughter of little Alexander and Christina. One
looking on might have seen a gentle puff of
breeze waft across their mother's cheek, rippling
a blonde curl, as she lay, serene and comfortable,
on the powdery sand.

The sun appeared to be a weight on her breast,
almost a physical presence, sensual and warm,
and she seemed to sigh and submit her body to
its healing. The sand underneath, soft and
malleable, was toasty as the bread ovens of

some French peasant. It baked her body through, perhaps draining away the excitement and tenseness of some late night party she and Ari might have thrown at the villa the night before.

The parties were legendary affairs; everyone came to them, Prince Ranier, famous French actors and artists, jet-setters from all over the world. Aristotle Onassis was renown for bringing forth bottle after bottle of wine to his guests, the dusty, yellowed labels proclaiming some priceless 1888 Brunello from the fabled vineyards of Tuscany, or his own favorite, Dom Perignon.

Laden with fresh-cut flowers rushed up the coastline from the enormous commercial gardens at Nice, the chateau might be perfumed by roses and carnations, alternately scented with pungent platters of lobster and violettes des roches fresh from the cool waters of the Mediterranean, and sumptuous tureens of bouillabaisse, simmering with the delectable fragrances of saffron, thyme, bay leaves, orange peel, fennel, tomatoes, onions, garlic and olive oil.

Down on the beach, Tina might stretch like some lithe kitten and blink sleepily, sitting up and shading her eyes to where the youngsters splashed happily.

At her beckoning, Christina and Alexander would plunge through the water toward their young and beautiful mother, dripping cold water over her sun-steamy skin. She would yelp and laugh, tackling them, rolling over and over on the beach until their brown bodies were powdered, looking for all the world like human sandpaper.

Finally, roughhousing over, the attendant maid would rinse the children's bodies and wrap them firmly in thick white towels, and lead them, objecting all the way, up the rocky hill to the villa for much needed naps.

Tina might roll over and watch them, then reach out her hand for the frosted glass which her maid had brought, licking her parched lips in thirsty anticipation. Fresh flowers might peep over the glass, yellow and red blossoms hiding chunks of pineapple and bananas picked that morning and flown in by seaplane for her pleasure. She would sip deeply the combination of fresh-squeezed lemons and oranges, also plucked that morning and sailed the few miles up the coast from the legendary orchards of Menton, where, it was whispered, Adam and Eve settled after their expulsion from Eden as the next best place to paradise.

With what appeared to be a contented sigh, Mrs. Onassis might head up the hill to the beautiful Chateau de la Croe, waving to Ari and his guests, some playing tennis on the wide courts, some wandering about the fountains dotting the twenty-five acres of carefully manicured lawns, arching their streams high into the air, and sprinkling down in a thousand sun-washed diamonds.

Deep in the enormous villa, one can only guess at Tina's afternoon. Perhaps she rushed to her private apartment, and into her enormous fabled bath, walled with mirrors over and around a finely-veined black marble floor. The beautiful young woman might drop her bikini on the floor and step into the swan-shaped tub, already filled with steaming water and scented oils. The solid gold faucets would glimmer in the mirror's reflection, and for her fair beauty, Tina would look very much a Greek goddess, at home in her fabled palace on Mt. Olympus.

Wrapping a thick towel about her, she could enter a private salon and press a button at the side of the door. At her touch, the ceiling would shudder and swing back, spilling in the Mediterranean sky. She might stand there bathed in the sun, inhaling deeply of the crisp air, then, kneeling, lie down on the plush carpet, falling into a gentle sleep as she sunbathed inside her own opulent retreat like some Oriental harem favorite.

Three short years later in 1954, Onassis' archrival, Stavros Niarchos, was to buy this legendary Chateau de la Croe for a paltry $575,000.00, banishing Ari and Tina from this azure paradise. They would be forced to take "refuge" in one of the dozens of Onassis' other homes around the world, or in the opulence of the newly purchased yacht, *Christina.* Or, back to Onassis' private island, Skorpios, which he had carved from a single uninhabitable rock, bulldozing hills and valleys, streams and waterfalls, spraying the entire island first with insecticide so that not one stinging, buzzing insect was left to mar the tranquillity of the island. By now, Skorpios was fully planted, laden with sweetly-scented flowers, olive trees, and groves of lemons and oranges, punctuated here and there by a pungent eucalyptus. For a man of unlimited wealth, expulsion from one paradise merely sends him speedily to numberless others.

Niarchos, in the meantime, was busy filling the Chateau de la Croe with part of his fifty million dollar collection of Van Goghs, Renoirs, Cezannes, Gauguins, and other Old Masters, and with fabulous antiques and silver bought from the estates of impoverished aristocrats.

Apparently, however, Niarchos' idea of buying the chateau was merely to sting his rival, for Niarchos and his wife reportedly rarely stayed there, consigning it, instead, to be a sumptuous playground for good friends!

Multiple dwellings have always been a necessity for the super-rich. J. P. Morgan's London servants, for example, were under strict instructions to turn down his finely-spun linen every night and to place a tumbler of warm milk on his nightstand, knowing all the while that the man was thousands of miles away at another palatial home across the Atlantic. As every loyal Boy Scout knows, it's good to be prepared.

No matter where the super-rich live, opulence is always the theme. The Jay Gould family's main home, *Lyndhurst*, was a Gothic mansion enthroned on a grass covered hill in the midst of five hundred acres of rolling woods, reflecting Jay Gould's passion for the beauties of nature. Surrounded by guards and gateways, the estate encompassed a yacht-landing, a swimming pool and bowling alley for the pleasure of the family and their guests, plus stables of fine horseflesh and equally magnificent carriage houses. Servant quarters were also located on the grounds, though, to be sure, well away from the

11

family mansion with its ivy-covered belfry.

Jay Gould's obsession for orchids was reflected in a series of interconnecting greenhouses, full of huge, lush ferns, palms, two thousand species of brilliant azaleas and over eight thousand orchids. His love of gardening was shown by the fact that the greenhouses covered far more ground than did the main house! It was, in fact, the largest private greenhouse in the world. Roses were ensconced in a room all their own, growing together in a wonderful riot of color. Each successive room held its own species of flower, and one could walk through the conservatory and find his way merely by the wonderful scent, first of roses, then carnations, on and on, room by room, till finally one came to the delicate feathery fragrance of orchids filling his nostrils.

In later years, Jay Gould's son, George, built his own home, *Georgian Court*, in Lakewood, New Jersey. This thirty room mansion, set in a framework of tall Tamarack pines, was the epitome of elegance. However, one pleasant summer day during a lawn party bedizened with champagne and parasols, it began to rain, forcing the guests indoors. George considered the party ruined and himself in disgrace, and family legend has it that he vowed it would never happen again. Mere vagaries of weather mean nothing to a rich man.

George Gould built the *Casino*, an enormous amphitheatre with a playing field the size of Madison Square Garden, complete with arching balconies where guests could sit in padded, roofed comfort, and watch their host play polo sitting on the finest ponies in the East.

Incredibly, the *Casino* also enclosed a life-size chess board where servants, dressed in medieval finery, portrayed kings and pawns and bishops, standing stiffly at attention, moving according to the chess master's calls.

If the guests tired of polo and chess, a whole circus might be brought into the ring for their private enjoyment, acrobats whirling from swing to swing, clowns employing their age-old comedic routines.

Bored with group entertainments, guests could retire to hit balls around the tennis courts, bowl in any one of three alleys, play a gentlemanly game of billiards, splash happily about in the massive pool, or steam party-knotted muscles to grateful relaxation in an elaborately appointed Turkish bath.

Of course, to complete the evening, he could tumble into bed in one of the twenty guest rooms right there in the *Casino*, and sleep until he was finished, awakening to the rejuvenation of steaming coffee in porcelain cups.

More fantastic even than the Gould's home was *Biltmore*, George W. Vanderbilt's castle built on 130,000 acres near Asheville, North Carolina, in the Blue Ridge Mountains. In preparation for the mammoth task of building his dream, Vanderbilt waded through volumes on landscape gardening, architecture, and forestry. In addition, he surrounded himself with thousands of European experts on the subjects, establishing the first forestry work ever done in the United States and employing more people than the U.S. Department of Agriculture!

Vanderbilt believed that an estate should be functional as well as beautiful, and the property reflects that viewpoint, even today. The family has since given 119,000 acres of the original 130,000 to the government. The gift is now known as Mt. Pisgah National Forest, a mountainous region blanketed with trees of breathtaking beauty. Many times the area is covered by a hazy quilt of blue fog, and the trees reach out, almost surrealistically, like a Chinese brush painting on rice paper.

As important to Vanderbilt as the incredible beauty was the conservation of land. When he began his project, much of the soil was worn out from generations of overfarming. His foresters cleared and replanted, with the result that the land has been given back its productivity and stands lush and full as virgin forest. *Biltmore* also encompassed a 1500-purebred Jersey farm, which, even today, provides employment and a solid financial base for the surrounding towns, and a marketplace for over three hundred other dairy farms in the region.

The Vanderbilt home is a monument to a man of aesthetic sensibilities, who sought to surround himself with the glories of God's nature, in harmony with its beauty, always remembering his responsibility to conserve and rebuild.

To enter the estate, a guest drives down a three mile road lined with mountain laurel and pine, undergirded with the splashy colors of rhododendrons. Deer wander and graze, freely, unafraid, on the slopes, adding to the serenity of the sylvan setting.

The avenue to the mansion itself is lined with tulip trees which, in springtime, burst forth with enormous pink and ruby blossoms, holding out their arms in welcome to a travel-weary guest. From the mammoth beveled-glass arched front doors, great stone lions overlook the famous grey stone retaining wall, its zig-zag architecture a Zorro slash in the hillside.

Inside, the manor house unfolds, with every step, a new delight; up the great curving staircase like the inside of a chambered nautilus; to the dining room with, not one, but three side-by-side fireplaces, taller than a man, stretching the entire width of the room. A sitting room's fireplace is framed by blue faience on the white mantel like some exquisite Grecian urn, mirrored in the polished hardwood floors which are spotted here and there with ancient Oriental carpets.

The library, pictured in all its heavy opulence in Peter Sellers' critically acclaimed movie, *Being There*, is lined two floors high with gold engraved books. Its black marble sills, carved with vining leaves, are a visual witticism above the red silk damask chairs where Peter Sellers, as Chauncey Gardener, sat as he discussed with "President Bobby" the "growing seasons of economics."

But if the interior seems sometimes a trifle cold in its massiveness, the gardens are a tribute to serenity. White Corinthian columns support heavy beams, dripping in purple wisteria, so deep and cool that even on the hottest day, they provide a summer hideaway by a tinkling pool.

English ivy climbs up the walls, overlaid with climbing roses like a colorful Italian mosaic. Down by the bass pond, a waterfall spills over onto rocks below, splashing onto a cypress' gnarled roots. Flowers continually bloom all during the long North Carolina summer; azaleas line the walking paths; over seven thousand roses grace the Rose Garden. The enormous greenhouse, glowing like some emerald-cut jewel, presides over the Italian garden, overlooking the mountains fading away into the blue haze of Mt. Pisgah.

To some people, these pastoral pleasures are the most important of all. Back in the 1920's, Mr. Paul D. Cravath, a New York attorney of great wealth, built himself a dream home on Long Island. After living there some time, he realized something very important was missing. What was wanted most, he felt, was a brook running through his living room. Yes, that would be perfect. What kind of a brook, the architect wanted to know. One that mutters, babbles, murmurs, or ripples?

Wrinkling his eyebrows in thoughtful anticipation, Mr. Cravath pondered, then smiled. He'd have all four, thank you. This simple pleasure added another $75,000 to the cost of his dream home.

After Count Boni de Castelane married Anna Gould, he built a pleasure dome the Kublai Khan would have loved. Costly white marble covered even the floors of the cellars, pantries, and kitchens. De Castelane reportedly explained that he loved to take ladies on tours of the house because the whispering of their long silken gowns on the marble sounded "almost exactly similar to waves breaking gently on the seashore."

A man's castle should be the place to indulge all his fancies, and, if the money is there, he need not be denied any of them, however outlandish they may seem to others.

Dr. Preston Pope Satterwhite, during the 1930's, built one of the largest apartments ever, right on Fifth Avenue in New York. Never one to be bored, he planned for sixty rooms, each one decorated in a different period of history. Mrs. Satterwhite could walk from an Indian throne room to a heavy English Jacobean dining hall, have breakfast in a dainty Queen Anne nook and then retire to a music room of soaring Moorish arches in deep wine paisley mosaics. Suiting her mood, she could luxuriate in the splendor of France's Louis XIV, or rest her sated eyes in a charming Cape Cod cubbyhole.

Shortly after the Satterwhite's moved into this fun house, Mrs. Satterwhite is supposed to have invited a friend for lunch. A stiff and pompous butler marched in to announce that luncheon would be served in the Sheraton gallery. The good woman is reported to have smiled and turned to lead her guest into the meal, when she suddenly frowned and turned back to the butler. "Where *is* it?" she asked, totally perplexed.

One of the great Silver Kings of the West, James C. Flood, built a second "modest" little home in Menlo Park, California. It was an amazement of turrets and gables and triple columns, with so much gingerbread that it earned the name "Flood's Wedding Cake." And, indeed, it looked precisely like an exquisite spun sugar house one might find in a fairy tale, or hiding inside a sugar Easter egg. So much carpeting was required that Flood's supplier found it more convenient to set up a store on the West coast rather than having to order everything from New York!

Physical infirmities can be easily accommodated with money. Mrs. Edward Doheny of Mexican Petroleum Company fame was quite blind, but she was intensely sensitive about her so-called handicap. Ramps were installed up steps and over door sills so she could enjoy her home unhampered by clutching helping hands. One of her greatest joys was a high-ceilinged greenhouse filled with tall trees and ferns as well as her extensive collection of orchids. Ma D, as she was lovingly called, ordered a long sterling centerpiece on the dining table filled every day with fresh orchids from the conservatory. Touching them gently, Ma D would learn the names of each in turn from a servant. That night, her guests would be amazed as she rattled off each variety's name of the flowers she loved but could not see.

Sometimes an opulent home can be an object lesson. John D. Rockefeller, Jr., wanted to teach his children the value of money, and to not let the family's vast wealth spoil them. Each child had to earn his spending money, polishing shoes or working in the vast gardens, or sometimes just swatting flies. However much each child earned, he was expected to keep a ledger, carefully entering money earned and money spent. Any child who could not account for every penny at the end of the week was fined a nickel; any child whose ledger was in perfect order earned an extra five cents.

Of all the Rockefeller's homes, the estate at Pocantico was the most opulent. This beautiful 3,500 acre retreat, five times the size of Central Park, was specifically reserved for weekends and vacations. With its richness, it is almost as though John Rockefeller were showing his children that if they could learn to restrain and control their spending, the wealth would always be there for them to truly enjoy.

Summers were a magic time there, as family legend has it, full of horseback riding and roaming the woods searching for baby bunnies and fawn. At the end of a long afternoon, often a rhythmic, scratchy whir and the thudding, cracking sound of ice being hammered in a gunny sack brought the children running. Under one of the thick shade trees, a tub of home-made ice cream was being turned, and the boys would jostle to see who would be first to stand on top, holding the freezer in place as the dasher slowly revolved through the sweet thick cream. Finally, too heavy to turn another half-stroke, Mrs. Rockefeller would scrape off the cracked ice and black-spotted salt, as the children waited, spoons poised, for the first delicious mouthful of the soft ice cream.

Girlfriends coming to visit daughter Babs could escape from her brothers' teasing by hiding in the apartment-sized playhouse, no doubt decorated in the whimsical fairy-tale fashion any little girl might dream about.

The boys had their own playhouse, a two-story gymnasium, where they could swim, or bowl, or elbow each other in a feisty game of basketball or squash. Tennis was a favorite game, and, if it rained or got too hot, the children merely had to move from the outdoor courts to the indoor ones. The playhouse gymnasium was big enough to throw lavish parties, with the Rockefeller teenagers and their friends dancing to big bands especially brought from New York by their dad.

Pocantico was the heart's home for the Rockefeller's, the place one thinks of at Christmas. So treasured was the estate that one day, when David Rockefeller was walking with his fiancee on the carefully manicured grounds, he noticed she had carelessly tossed down the peels from an orange she was eating. He turned back and picked up every peel, reportedly admonishing her, "We *never* litter the ground."

Not a piece of paper, not an orange peel disgraced the eighteenth century tiered gardens, so carefully planted with sweetly-scented flowers and French orange trees, the rock fountains pouring over into the little brook, the hills sloping down gently to the Hudson River, flowing serenely by.

Perhaps John D. Rockefeller's lessons in appreciation of money worked after all.

While some of the super-rich built opulent homes to cater to their tastes in nature, or parties, or athletics, William Astor lived out his passion for history. The American Astor, on one of his countless visits to the centuries' old lands of Europe, traveled in great luxury throughout England. To his mind, obsessed with history and reveling in the rich fabric of England's heroic past, Britain seemed a wondrous country in which to live. What remained now was to find the perfect spot.

He roamed from place to place, seeing the green misty isles of the 19th century with his eyes, but, with his heart, envisioning the long-dead past.

On the daffodil-covered Isles of Scilly, he may have remembered the legend of King Arthur's last battle here against Mordred, with Merlin's incantation sinking the fabled land of Lyonesse, drowning the traitors as the Knights of the Round Table watched in victory. In London, he may have recalled the fierce warrior queen, Boudicca, savagely leading the Celtic onslaught against Roman Londinium astride a raging stallion; or visited the Tower of London with its tragic history, perhaps feeling the presence of Sir Walter Raleigh or Guy Fawkes, or walked with the ghosts of Anne Boleyn and Catherine Howard, or heard the undying, faith-filled words of Sir Thomas More as that great man refused to compromise his belief in God for his life. At Runnymede, he could have seen in his mind's eye a sullen King John signing the historic Magna Charta surrounded by adamant knights. And, at Stratford-On-Avon, Astor may have watched as Shakespeare penned sonnets in charming, ivy-covered eggstone cottages.

Someplace there had to be a place for this American millionaire to make his British home. All he had to do was find it.

Then one day, traveling through Kent, William Astor stumbled upon a neglected and desolate castle, its empty mullioned windows staring out like sad eyes. Picturesque ivy clawed into the mortar, crumbling and pulling down the ancient cream-colored stones. Weeds and debris clogged the moat.

But something about the place attracted Astor and he began to ask questions. Yes, he was told by a local historian, that castle was special. There, in a quiet alcove, surrounded by softly-rubbed oak, Henry the Eighth wooed Anne Boleyn, beseeching her love with what he perceived to be sweet ballads of undying passion. Finally, giving in to the overwhelming pressures of her all-powerful liege, Anne married the corpulent king, eventually losing her head in the process.

Now it was whispered, here the historian lowered his voice, that Anne Boleyn's ghost sorrowfully roams the corridors of the broken castle, and, during the Christmas season, when all the English countryside is alive with joy and feasting, one might hear Anne singing, in a sad minor key, songs of her lost innocence.

This legend was too much for William Astor's history-buff mind. He bought the ancient Hever Castle on the spot, and proceeded to spend a reported ten million Victorian dollars to restore the home of Anne Boleyn's ghost.

The leaded, bubbled glass was polished and

replaced where needed. The moat was dredged and deepened, it soon ran clean and blue. Stones and mortar were repaired, and the oaken walls were buffed to their original splendor.

Astor also drained marshes and changed the course of the nearby river to suit his own purposes, much to the chagrin and astonishment of local Englishmen. He had in mind to bring in farm animals to complete the pastoral scene of his castle, but they must not live in just any old barn. Indeed not. They would live in accordance with the splendor of Henry the Eighth. The American multimillionaire built a dairy with a floor of Italian mosaic, and the cows were to live in barns lined with expensive tiles of cream and Hershey brown. Even the pig sty was built of finest English oak!

Lovely Italian gardens soon surrounded the castle, and deer roamed freely within the confines of their own special forest. Here William Astor was able to live, his dream come true, completely immersed in the living history of England.

2

Spending Sprees

Howard Hughes' Ice Cream Caper

The young reporter perched on the edge of his chair. This interview meant everything to him. Stranded in Paris, his funds were almost gone. But, with one timely stroke of luck, he had been able to gain audience with the owner of the New York Herald, James Gordon Bennett. If this eccentric millionaire were impressed, there might be a post for him on Bennett's French subsidiary, the Paris Herald, and there would be money again for croissants and a room overlooking the Left Bank.

But something clearly was wrong. Bennett kept twisting in his seat and frowning, clutching at his clothing like the uncomfortable man in an underwear commercial. He was paying no attention whatsoever to the young man's pleas.

Finally, in total frustration, Bennett stood up, huffed, and dragged out an enormous roll of bills. With an exasperated grunt, he pitched the offending lump into the blazing fireplace. In astonishment and consternation, the young reporter cried out and raced to the fire, raking out the blackened wad of money. Juggling this hot potato, he rushed it back across the room to its owner.

Bennett is said to have stared up at the young man, his upper lip curling in disgust. "That's exactly where I wanted it," he is reported to have sneered, tossing the bundle back into the flames.

Well, the super-rich can do whatever they want with their money, although burning it admittedly seems a trifle wasteful. The range of spending can span the whole range of human imagination—whatever the mind of man can enjoy, he can figure out a way to spend a lot of money on.

Some time after Madeline Astor's husband died heroically on the ill-fated Titanic, she appeared before the probate judge. Please *do* something, she begged, there simply wasn't enough money for her to get by.

The judge looked over her petition. Well, what necessities did she need?

Mrs. Astor looked indignant. Why, clothing for the children, of course.

Upon further examination, her request for more ermine robes and fur-trimmed baby clothing was found to be too foolish to be believed, and the judge refused, shaking his legal head in wonder.

But jewels, those fancy baubles for fingers and ears and throats, have always retained that special bit of magic, both for who could buy the most, who could buy the largest, and who could display them most effectively. After all, one doesn't outgrow jewels the way babies outgrow buntings.

Mrs. Potter Palmer, fond recipient of her husband's millions, was accustomed to wearing most of her jewels at a single stagger. When she was fully loaded, so to speak, the lady wobbled as though drunken from the sheer weight of her diamonds.

Mrs. John Drexel also favored a jewel-encrusted body. She devised a type of "Sam Browne belt," one of those criss-crossed cartridge belts beloved by Mexican bandits, and studded it with precious gems, strutting about like a Pancho Villa laden with diamonds instead of bullets.

When this ostentation became too prosaic, ladies began to go to opposite extremes. One grand dame appeared at the opera wearing one single perfect diamond, followed by her maid, totally laden by every gem the lady ever owned.

Mrs. Frederick Vanderbilt went her one better. Appearing one night in a string of pearls that nearly dragged the floor, she artfully played with an enormous ruby by kicking it in front of her like a child playing kick the can.

But, in the epitome of understatement, Grace Vanderbilt often appeared in a shimmering gold lame' Worth gown, her only jewelry an exquisite gold charm bracelet from which dangled five golden charms. Inside each of the charms lay the key to one of her five gem-stuffed jewelry boxes.

The world's unqualified queen of jewelry was Evalyn Walsh McLean, who, in her time, owned the most fabulous gems in the world, including the Star of India and the Hope Diamond.

Evalyn's consuming passion for gems began on her honeymoon, when both her father and the groom's father gave the young couple a wedding gift of $100,000.00 apiece. Now, in those days of pre-double digit inflation, $200,000.00 should have been ample for any couple to enjoy a European honeymoon. However, no one reckoned on Evalyn's obsession with precious gems. One day, while visiting the fabled vaults of Cartier's, the new Mrs. McLean spotted a jewel which she reportedly admitted "made spots in front of my eyes." One can almost picture the young bride's blood pulsing harder and her breathing becoming labored as she gazed on the Star of the East, an exquisite 92.5 carat pear-shaped diamond dangling from a 34 karat emerald and topped by a shimmering pearl of 32.5 karats. The gallant groom leapt to his bride's rescue. This, after all, was the perfect wedding gift for his beloved. Without a moment's hesitation, Mr. McLean bought the precious toy for $120,000.00, then wired home to Dad for the money to pay it off.

That honeymoon trip was even more fateful, however, when Evalyn and Ned were presented to the Sultan Abdul-Hamid in Constantinople. Even in all of Evalyn's richly ornamented life, she had never seen opulence like this.

The Sultan sat on plush pillows in the oriental palace, an enormous dark emerald dangling from the top of his fez. Ned and Evalyn sat beside him, their eyes widening in delight as coffee was served, strong and steaming, in the

27

daintiest, fragile porcelain cups, resting comfortably in holders of braided gold studded with diamonds.

Later, they followed the Sultan down the palace corridors to his harem, where his ladies lounged in oriental luxury, dressed in filmy veils and wondrous jewels. Imagine Mrs. McLean's gasp as she spotted a mammoth blue stone, the most beautiful diamond in the world. One suspects it was all she could do to keep from snatching it from the throat of the Sultan's favorite and racing away from the palace, angry eunuchs in mad pursuit. Little did she know then that this beautiful Hope Diamond would one day fall with the government of the Sultan, and drift on the dim backroads of the black-market, to reach Paris and her own itching fingers.

To celebrate this acquisition of acquisitions, Evalyn threw a party to end all parties, sitting in state with the fabulous stone freshly wreathed in white diamonds and hanging on a diamond chain about her neck, and herself framed with four thousand yellow lilies flown in from London especially for the occasion. The dinner alone set Ned McLean back $40,000 in pre-Depression currency. But, for the Hope Diamond, no less auspicious premiere would do.

All this is not to insinuate that gentlemen do not find diamonds and gemstones just as fascinating as their wives and sisters. Ned Green, for example, is reported to have bought over ten million dollars in gems during his lifetime, usually while double-parked outside the jewelry store. To ensure getting a bargain, Green hired his own appraiser who traveled with him at all times, just in case Ned ran across a good buy.

A trip to Ned Green's home must have been a real experience. In pre-indoor plumbing Victorian days, Ned's bathrooms were the zenith of luxury, containing the ultimate chamber pot, encrusted with diamonds! But even Ned Green may have gone too far the day he brought home to his lady the gem-studded chastity belt!

If Evalyn Walsh McLean was the queen of jewels, then Diamond Jim Brady was the undisputed king. Diamond Jim owned whole collections of pearls, rubies, emerald, sapphires, black opals, turquoise, amethysts, coral, plus the pale beauty of moonstones just now coming back into popularity. After acquiring too many diamonds to comfortably wear, Brady had many of them set into his legendary "transportation set," shirt and vest studs, cuff links and lapel buttons all shaped in the forms of locomotives, airplanes, cars and bicycles.

Along with jewels, bicycles seemed to have been Brady's obsession, and it was inevitable he should find a way to combine these passions. Once, according to tradition, he had twelve steel bicycles frames electroplated with pure gold, with a diamond here and there on the handlebars for "class." These were merely his everyday wheels. The top of the class vehicle was specially made as a gift from Diamond Jim to his friend, the famous Lillian Russell. Miss Russell's bicycle had an especially heavy coat of gold with mother-of-pearl handlebars. Sapphires, diamonds, rubies, and emeralds were affixed to every spoke in the wheels, flashing in the sun with every revolution with all the brilliance of tiny stained glass windows!

Like the golden bicycle of Miss Russell, gifts to friends can assume mythic proportions. During one luxurious expedition on a private railroad car, J. P. Morgan ordered the route diverted through Seattle so he could usher his friends into a famous fur store, allowing them to pick out a sumptuous coat or rug as a special present from him.

During the famous parties of the rich, expensive gifts were always given as favors to their guests. During one such party, Grace Vanderbilt gave exquisite little clocks studded with gems, and purses of the softest suede adorned with a clasp of sapphires and turquoise to her lady guests. Glove-soft leather cases bound in silver were given to each man to hold his personal supply of postage stamps.

In an equally magnanimous gesture, Grace's mother-in-law, during lunch with her son, Reggie Vanderbilt, and his new bride, Gloria, asked why Reggie had not yet given his wife her pearls.

Reggie, on the defensive, insisted that he refused to buy his wife a cheap string of pearls and could not afford the kind he had in mind.

The old woman is reported to have snapped

her fingers and summoned the maitre d', asking for a pair of scissors. "All Vanderbilt women have pearls," she is supposed to have huffed, clipping off close to a third of the immense string about her neck. The portion of the necklace handed to Gloria Vanderbilt was reported to have been worth about $70,000 at the time.

Perhaps the most interesting spending sprees involve the arts. Alfred Rothschild's passion was music. He kept an entire symphony orchestra *on hand* just so he could conduct one of Beethoven's stirring symphonies or the measured tread of a Bach fugue each evening after supper. Even today, Rothschild legend glitters around "Alfred's baton," a resplendent ivory wand encircled by diamonds.

The Greek shipbuilder, Stavros Niarchos, owns one of the world's finest collections of art. It is said the Greek loves to surround himself with art just because it makes him happy, and the fact that his collection is reportedly worth over fifty million dollars apparently matters not a whit. That is easy to understand, especially considering the paintings he owns; Botticelli's ladies, soft, round women with pale hair cascading down in gentle curls; Titian's luminous chestnut hair seeming to glow from within; the heavy richness of the Flemish Madonnas contrasting spectacularly with the delicacy of Degas' ballerinas, whose tutus seem ephemeral and unreal; Rembrandt's majestic nudes, whose bodies emerge into light from deepest shadow; Durer's portraits in subtle colors so real that they seem to breathe life from the canvas; the vivid colors of Cezanne's landscapes, and the even more intense energies of Van Gogh, whose bold brush strokes and vibrant colors broke through old realism and left the art world shaken by his flames of madness. Niarchos reportedly often stalked a desired painting or collection of paintings for years, and, when it was finally run to earth, no price would be too high for its acquisition.

After J. P. Morgan purchased a famous collection of exquisite Chinese porcelains, he learned the collection was incomplete. "I trust, then," he is reported to have commanded, "you will complete it for me." Even back then, at the turn of the century, the porcelains were priceless, and the art dealer must have gasped at the realization of what his commissions were going to be worth.

Years later, after Morgan's death, the collection came up for sale. The young John D. Rockefeller, Jr., with a passionate fondness for porcelains, found himself with a once in a lifetime opportunity to purchase a portion of the collection. In 1915, Rockefeller had not yet received his inheritance and had to ask his father to advance him the paltry million or so dollars. Father Rockefeller, ever the pragmatic businessman, did not share his son's enthusiasm for things of artistic beauty, and refused the request. Indignant, young Rockefeller wrote an angry note, reminding his father that he never once squandered money on many "vices" of the super-rich such as yachts or racehorses.

Porcelains were his only hobby, he wrote, and after all, he had never before asked his father for *anything*. True, true, Father Rockefeller could not deny this; Junior got his loan, and the precious porcelains were his.

Often spending sprees reflect the oddities and quirks of the millionaries. For example, Vincent Astor was very sensitive about his feet which, from childhood on, had pointed outward causing him to walk in an awkward fashion. Identifying strongly with the little Charlie Chaplin-esque penguin walk, Vincent had the penguin motif placed on everything he owned, from diamond cuff links to silk ties and gold wristwatches. Even his cigarettes were especially imprinted with the funny little bird.

The Baron Philippe Rothschild, avid believer in "early to bed, early to rise," despised to wait even a moment after guests left a dinner party to hit the sack. He ordered his tailor to design the softest, silken shirt for his tuxedo, to be used also as a sleeping shirt. Carelessly tossing off the pants and jacket, Philippe could be asleep before the last guest rolled out of the driveway!

Some quirks reverse themselves and take on odd measures of economies. Aristotle Onassis, all during his life, refused to wear an overcoat, and never once even owned one. His rationale was that he was always chauffeur-driven and thus only a few steps from a warm limousine to wherever he wanted to go. He explained to one friend that he often visited a dozen or more nightclubs or restaurants every day. In his capacity as one of the super-rich, he would be expected to tip lavishly, probably at least $5.00, every time he would check his coat. Additionally, because of his status, the topcoat would have to be very expensive, vicuna or mink at the very least, and he would be forced to insure the thing. Onassis figured that doing without the topcoat saved him over $20,000.00 a year!

Even annoyances can be cured with liberal doses of money. Once when Neily Vanderbilt was ill with peritonitis, his fever ranged from 104 to 105 degrees for several days on end. The noise of hooves clattering in the street outside their New York apartment was disturbing his feverish rest, so his wife, Grace, nearly sick with worry herself, merely called the mayor of New York City. Within the hour, workmen were busy spreading straw on the cobblestones under their windows. The noise ceased.

John M. Longyear, iron magnate, built himself a home of impeccable taste and culture, reflecting his insatiable reading habits. His library was packed from floor to ceiling with fine literature and Mr. Longyear, then retired, loved to spend long, quiet afternoons reading the wonderful stories.

His peace was soon shattered when the railroad tracks of the Duluth, Mesabi and Iron Range Railroad slithered by just underneath his library windows. The smoke stacks of the locomotives spewed out soot which soon settled indiscriminately over Longyear's oak and leather interior.

In a fury, Mr. Longworth fought the railroad clear to the Michigan Supreme Court, but there was no other suitable right of way, and, for once, all Longworth's money could not keep out the noise and dirt of civilization.

But this old man was not yet beaten, not by a long shot. Get photographers in here, he roared. One can imagine his raised eyebrow, the jutting of his chin. Every room, every single tree and bush, every fountain, every building down to the last greenhouse was photographed, and, before long, the *entire* estate was loaded onto the offending railroad cars and whisked off to a quieter neighborhood. Soon workmen had reconstructed everything, manor house, greenhouse, fountains, gardens and all, and Mr. Longyear once again sat in his library, happily reading, with no more than a passing huff at the railroads.

One of Las Vegas' favorite legends tells about Howard Hughes calling one of the local television stations with a request. Run movies all night, he ordered, I want to see them all night. The answer was no, it was just too expensive to show movies all night when not enough people watched. Of course, the station manager hinted, if Mr. Hughes *really* wanted movies all night, perhaps he could just buy the station. . . .

All right, buy it, came the succinct command. And movies were run all night, every night, according to Hughes' desire. People of Las Vegas became exceedingly weary of seeing *Ice Station Zebra* on the tube.

Hughes was the most bizarre of all multi-millionaires. Tales of his incredible and fantastic behavior have reached epic proportions. Perhaps the best known story of what money can buy is what has been called his "secrecy machine." Once, to prevent the possibilities of bomb threats or kidnappings, Hughes ordered whole fleets of old beat-up Chevrolets parked in airport garages around the country for his use. Who would notice an old Chevrolet? And, even if they did, how could a possible kidnapper or bomber determine which old Chevrolet Hughes would use next? Seems reasonable.

Years later, long after Hughes was incapable of moving from place to place except by stretcher, the Chevrolets were remembered, their batteries long since dead and the tires completely flat from years of air leakage.

In Hughes' later years, he often refused to eat. So, any time the weak and debilitated man requested food of any kind, his hirelings rushed to obtain it at any cost. One of Hughes' fancies was Baskin-Robbins ice cream, particularly the fruity goodness of banana nut. Gallons were kept on hand at all times, and dishes were brought to the eccentric nightly for what nourishment he would consent to take.

One day, it was discovered that the ice cream was almost gone. Get over to Baskin Robbins, one of the executives ordered, and get some more. Sorry, sir, the underling was told at the ice cream shop, that flavor has been discontinued.

One can imagine the horrified, stricken look on his face. No more banana nut? Impossible! What were they to do?

A hasty phone call was made to Baskin-Robbins' head office in California. Can we get more? Can a special order be made up?

Oh, yes, of course, sir, came the reply. But we can only make it up in orders of three hundred and fifty gallons. Not bothering to worry about where in the world they would store three hundred and fifty gallons of ice cream in the Desert Inn Hotel, the go-ahead was given.

Soon three hundred fifty delicious gallons of banana nut ice cream were delivered. *Now* was the time to worry about where to put the rapidly melting goodies.

The Hughes' executives approached the hotel's chef. Could they use the hotel's freezer? The chef exploded. Where was he going to put the hotel's food? Finally, pacified with green stuff, food was shuffled around and three hundred fifty gallons of ice cream was stored away.

At least they could relax now. They had enough banana nut to last for years! No doubt the executives felt very good about themselves.

That night, the traditional dish of banana nut ice cream was carried smugly, ceremoniously, into Hughes' presence. He looked down at it, then back to his employees. "Y'know," Hughes is reported to have said, "I really like this ice cream, but I'm kinda tired of it. It's time for a change. Let's try French Vanilla next."

3

Feasts and Fetes

Chocolates for Diamond Jim

The last time we saw the American newspaperman, James Gordon Bennett, he was
pitching an enormous wad of bills into the
flames before the horrified eyes of a penniless
American expatriot. Now we find him marching
determinedly towards his favorite restaurant,
his mind set on a savory plate of exquisite
Southdown mutton chops. This particular little
restaurant had, in the past few weeks, become
the hallmark of Bennett's Monte Carlo noon-
time. The delightful outdoor patio overlooked
the sumptuous blue of the Mediterranean
harbor below, filled with the tracery of sleek
yacht masts, and Bennett loved to take his
luncheon gazing down into the harbor.

He reached the restaurant to find the owner
cowering behind the counter, his face pale and
worried. Might Mr. Bennett consent to take his
mutton chops indoors today? The restauranteur
wrung his hands together like some washer-
woman squeezing water from overalls. As Mr.

Bennett could see, there were already patrons taking up the tiny outdoor tables.

Bennett turned around and glared at the interlopers. They poured another round of wine and lifted their glasses high, ignoring him, and continued with their serious merrymaking.

Would Mr. Bennett *mind*? Indeed he would! He wanted his mutton chops and he wanted them *now*. And he wanted them sitting at his usual table, overlooking the picturesque harbor.

With this, the restauranteur became even more agitated. He couldn't afford to lose his best customer, but it wasn't right to toss out the serious drinkers on their collective ears, either.

Suddenly, Bennett leaned forward and whispered to the shaken man conspiratorially. Might this restaurant be for sale? He pulled out a wad of bills. The offer was good for this moment only. Take it or leave it. The astonished owner glanced from Bennett's face to the bills and back again. Finally he gulped and took the money. The eating place forthwith belonged to Bennett. Within moments, the wealthy man was seated at his favorite table, peacefully looking out over his sunny domain; the incredulous drinkers were suddenly on the outside looking in. Within a few more moments, the chef strutted forth, carrying a fragrant platter of mutton chops. With incredible foresight, he had thrown the meat onto the fire the minute he saw Bennett stroll up. Just in case.

The succulent chops were excellent, as always, and Bennett savored each morsel. Finally, with every trace of the meal consumed, and feeling in a most expansive mood, Bennett rose to leave.

"Excellent," he is reported to have murmured to his waiter, dropping the keys to the restaurant into the astonished man's palm as a gratuity.

Shortly thereafter, the restaurant's sign was changed to read, "Ciro's," and thus began the tale of one of the most famous eating places in Europe. And one pleasant ending to the story: Bennett never again had to worry about getting a seat for his mutton chop meals.

Captain King of the famous Texas King Ranch had other ways of dealing with difficult restaurants. Once, while dining with friends in a swanky New Orleans dining room, one of his guests tried vainly to chew a tough bite of steak. The gallant Captain King raised his finger to summon the waiter. King family lore reports that the waiter, haughty, insisted, "Sorry, there is nothing I can do."

Indignant, Captain King then summoned the headwaiter, who turned out to be as obstinate and impolite as his underling.

Simmering now, the Captain, with all the dash of a true Texas son, strode across the street to another four-star restaurant and ordered a whole new meal for his entire party. "Bring it to me across the street," he ordered tersely to the astonished waiters, who did as they were bidden.

The headwaiter of the first restaurant was indignant. Clear the table? Indeed they would not. Why, the very idea, bringing in another chef's food to our beautiful dining room.

Drawing himself up to his full John Wayne height, Captain King grasped the linen tablecloth and yanked. Food, crystal, china, flowers and all crashed to the floor. "Serve it now!" he roared.

Chastened, and much subdued, the waiters scurried to serve the fresh food. Captain King is reported to have calmly settled back in his seat and continued with the fine conversation which had been so rudely interrupted.

Sometimes eating habits of the super-rich border on the bizarre. J. Pierpont Morgan loved to eat enormous breakfasts, often consisting of luscious fresh fruit, (not necessarily in season), delicate eggs, a steaming bowl of oatmeal swimming in thick cream, a generous bowl of hash, and a platter of crispy fried fish surrounded by a wreath of sliced red tomatoes.

If Morgan ate field-hand-sized breakfasts, his lunches were modest, maybe a turkey sandwich, or a plate of fresh peaches warm off the tree and smothered in sugar, with nothing more than a plain glass of water to wash them down. Perhaps the lightness of the lunch was in concession to his habit of gargantuan dinners, sometimes nine or ten courses at a time, each divided by an appropriate wine. The first course sometimes consisted of oysters, crab bisque, consomme' and various hors d'oeuvres, and then after a particulary fine German wine, a whole course of clams would be brought forth.

Another wine, and then an enormous platter of spring lamb, accompanied by tiny fresh peas and a special potato dish. After that, and another French wine, came terrapin. (Back in those days terrapin was not an endangered

41

species, although from its appearance on so many exclusive menus, the vastly wealthy may have single-handedly contributed to its demise!) With the terrapin came a serving of fresh, tart grapefruit soaked in Kirsch. *Groan*.

After yet another wine came a brace of canvasback ducks, fried hominy, and crispy celery. Then came the *(sigh)* dessert, an elegant parfait with assorted aged cheeses from all over the world, fruit, and demitasse cups filled with invigorating coffee. No doubt one needed the coffee after all that wine.

The gentlemen ended their repast with a giant Havana cigar and cognac in crystal snifters. One imagines Morgan and his guests tottering to the library in an almost drugged state, yet, from all reports, meals such as this were a common occurrence among the rich of the day.

The tale is told of Randolph Guggenheimer who threw a party one icy and unpleasant February night, transporting his guests to a gentle summer evening. Strolling into an elegant private restaurant, the guests shook the snow and ice from their shoulders and slippers, stepping through a trellis festooned with roses and enormous clumps of Hamburg grapes. It is reported that the grapes cost, in that pre-inflationary-spiral time, a handy $10.00 per bunch.

Wandering into the dining hall, the guests were greeted with the sight of precious orchids and American Beauty roses surrounding a twenty-foot long pool jutting down the length of the dining table. (The story is told that at an earlier dinner, a similar dining table pool was also filled with swans, but that, intrigued by the sumptuous smell of foie gras, the graceful birds decided to join the party, and flapped wet feathers all over the harried guests!) So, minus the swans, the guests sat down to a dinner with a menu similar to that of J. P. Morgan's. They tell us that it took several hours of intensive eating just to down all the delicacies of the evening.

In the contest of voracious gluttony, the undisputed king was Diamond Jim Brady. His normal meals have come down to us as epicurean legends. Even to fellow diners of the day, accustomed to three-hour feasts, Brady's eating marathons were an amazement. Fascinated observers would gather around just to watch him eat, and to place bets on whether Diamond Jim would collapse before the end of his Bacchanalia.

According to stories of the day, during one of these unabashed orgies of eating, Brady would swill down several *gallons* of freshly-squeezed orange juice, just for a start. He not only customarily ate every course of a twelve course meal, but often would consume several *extra* helpings of the main offerings. In one meal alone, a dozen-egg souffle, several broiled game birds, a large hunk of venison, a huge mutton, *and* often six dozen oysters might fall to his fork. And, at the very end, Brady would lovingly dip into a five pound box of the most delicious chocolates he could find, ecstatically downing nearly the whole thing.

The story is told that once, while in Boston, Diamond Jim came across some chocolates made by the tiny local shop of Page and Shaw. He enthusiastically devoured a whole five pound box and stamped his seal of approval on it by declaring them the best chocolates he ever ate. Drawing forth his business card, he ordered the entire stock sent to friends. The supplier was noticeably upset. Well, sir, he tried to explain, we have other regular customers. Page and Shaw was just a small operation. The man's face was sad. He hoped the big man understood.

Understand? The only thing Diamond Jim understood was that he couldn't have his candy. Drawing forth $150,000.00, he ordered the candy shop to increase operations, and to keep him supplied at all times with this incredible delicacy. It did.

Parties of the super-rich reach epic proportions, like Walt Disney's *Fantasia*. Newspapers of the day recounted one such party given by Mr. and Mrs. Bradley-Martin allowing all the working stiffs to enjoy the evening vicariously. Five enormous mirrors were draped with mauve orchids and plemusa vine, with roses of all shades, lilies-of-the-valley and orchids fairly upholstering the columns and walls. The newspaper described the artful display of mauve orchids, which streamed "carelessly to the floor, like the untied bonnet strings of a thoughtless child." Ah, those were the days of poetic editors!

No expense was too great to afford each guest the most enjoyable evening possible. During one party, Mrs. Bradley-Martin hired four hundred carriages to transport her guests home so that their own coachmen could go to their quarters and get some sleep.

Family history tells that, on the day of one of Grace Vanderbilt's fabulous parties, the florist might send over half a dozen shades of her favorite, the American Beauty rose. She would hold each up to her precious antique draperies, determining exactly the appropriate color before ordering them sent over and placed in huge stately vases. With her incredible memory for the smallest details, she also remembered, to a person, each guest's favorite sweet, and ordered it placed by his or her plate. It did not matter to her that she might have to order a dozen different types of candies to accommodate her friends. They were worth it.

Alfred Rothschild also felt his friends worthy of everything he could offer. A guest might be awakened by a stiff and solicitous butler, standing at attention with an enormous silver tray.

Rothschild lore indicates that the butler would offer, "Tea, coffee, or a ripe peach, sir?"

Perhaps the unsuspecting guest would choose tea. The butler, unperturbed, would respond, his hands full of three teapots, "Tea from China, India, or Ceylon, sir?"

At the guest's choosing, the butler again turned to his seemingly endless cart, bringing forth lemons, cream, and milk. Would the kind sir take any of these?

If the hapless guest chose milk or cream, the butler would solemnly intone, "Hereford,

Shorthorn, or Jersey?"

Rothschild guests were always made to feel this kind of special service. A headache was cured with a long carriage ride in the country, a cold treated with a medicine chest as extensive as the family wine cellar. Gifts were lavisly given all during the stay, and guests carried away precious mementoes of Alfred Rothschild's generosity.

This exuberant Rothschild enjoyed treating his guests to circuses, and often would appear in a carriage drawn by four zebras, drawing up short before his friends' plush seats, playing ringmaster and sporting, of all things, a pair of lavender kid gloves!

Another party, famous in its day and still gossiped about in the annals of party-giving, was the horseback dinner given by Mr. C.K.G. Billings. Guests arrived on their favorite steeds and sat astride during the whole of the meal, sampling goodies from trays set atop the pommels of their saddles. Lest the horses feel left out, oats were served during dessert, and a lively game of polo was enjoyed after men and horses had eaten their fill.

One of the most incredible parties of the day was given by Mrs. Vanderbilt, dubbed by the press "The Fete of Roses." She had become bored with what she termed "amateur musicals" and decided to import the hit musical "The Wild Rose" from its run on Broadway. One cannot even imagine how much it cost to close out a sell-out performance on Broadway and ship the entire troupe to Beaulieu, the family's mansion in Newport. But she did it.

The night of the party arrived, along with a mere two hundred of society's ritziest guests. Mrs. Vanderbilt had transformed her entire capacious lawn into a carnival, with games of chance and dancing girls for her guests' amusement. A red velvet carpet covered the grass, and a barn-red canopy sheltered the jamboree, lit up with tiny red lights.

At the stroke of midnight, the guests moved from the midway to Mrs. Vanderbilt's elegant outdoor lawn theatre. The hot August night faded away as the booming Atlantic surf crashed against the shore and sent salty breezes over the assembled, waiting crowd.

Soon, the velvet curtains parted and a snappy one-hour review of "The Wild Rose" was presented, to thunderous applause. Mrs. Vanderbilt then led her guests to supper, while an army of carpenters transformed the theatre stage into a ballroom. The guests danced until dawn, when they were offered a sunrise breakfast, lest they leave (heaven forbid) on an empty stomach.

Next day, the New York newspaper editors, hardened by having seen nearly everything, showed how impressed they were by the party. President Roosevelt, traveling about on trips of political consequence, was given one shabby column, while the description of Mrs. Vanderbilt's "Fete of the Roses" took four and a half columns!

Once, tiring of all the folderol of the ladies' parties, Ogden Reid devised one just for the gentlemen. He and a few friends would run down to North Carolina on a hunting trip. The city boys, not having any of the necessary accoutrements for duck hunting, sallied forth to Abercrombie and Fitch, buying up the finest English shotguns, expensive tweed hunting jackets, and rubber waders to keep their feet dry and warm.

Setting off in two of Reid's Rolls-Royces, the group unfortunately made a stop in Philadelphia to visit a friend, John T. Custus, who forthwith escorted his new guests to his private club. Three days of serious men's-clubbing set the party back nearly a week before the Rolls-Royce limousines rolled on again towards North Carolina and the duck blinds.

As the car passed through Washington, D.C., one gentleman mentioned that it would indeed be bad manners not to at least look in on the Washington correspondent of Reid's Herald Tribune, and the party halted once again. The correspondent, Ted Wallen, set up a little visit to see President Hoover at the White House, and off they trouped, in those days prior to security checks by the Secret Service, for an enjoyable evening with the country's chief executive.

At one o'clock in the morning, President Hoover insisted they stay the night, and he ordered pajamas brought out for his guests, who were soon lodged in the historic Lincoln bedroom and other rooms of the mansion.

Finally, heading south again, the safari reached North Carolina, only to discover, much to their chagrin, that the hunting season had ended only the day before. Apparently not even all of Reid's money could persuade the local warden to extend the season, and the Abercrombie and Fitch hunting gear never saw the light of the North Carolina marshes.

Costume parties were much loved. Indeed, the few parties ever attended by Howard Hughes were the annual costume parties given by his friend, William Randolph Hearst. The millionaire newspaperman arranged to transport Hughes and other top Hollywood stars of the day to famed San Simeon, high atop a cliff overlooking the Pacific Ocean, by way of luxurious private railroad cars.

Arriving at the incredible mansion, guests found it transformed into a magic kingdom of priceless antiques, with exotic zoo animals strolling about the grounds as if they owned the place. Giraffes, camels, zebras, and other fine specimens cavorted with the invited guests who were dressed in every manner of period history.

Earlier, during the Depression years, the Silver King James Flood decided to throw an immense costume party to enliven the flagging spirits of the day. His entire home was emblazoned with azaleas and fruit trees in full blossom.

The guests were arrayed in incredible variety; Flood's own son portrayed Popeye, the Sailor Man, and one lady arrived as Noah's Ark. Her blue gown, obviously representing water, was painted with all the pairs of animals, and she sported a hat shaped like the ark. A local newspaper described the chapeau as having Noah's three brothers in back and a dove perched on top in the front.

Silk and satin abounded in imitations of French royalty, contrasting sharply with the man who bounded into the ballroom as an old western prospector, dragging his own mule!

Flights of fancy soared on and on, each party building over the ones preceding it. In what he considered a stroke of genius, Mr. James Paul hit upon a terrific idea for the coming-out party of his daughter, Mary Astor Paul. He would import 10,000 butterflies from Brazil and fasten them in a bag near the ceiling, and, at the appropriate time, a servant would yank a string and the butterflies would spill out, fluttering gracefully throughout the ballroom, entrancing the guests with their brilliant colors and delicate flight. It sounded like a marvelous idea.

But, Mr. Paul forgot the one common-sense rule that heat rises, and, during the intensity of the evening, all the candles and the body heat of hundreds of guests took its toll upon the unfortunate little beauties. The string was pulled, the bag opened, and 10,000 dead, sodden butterflies dumped themselves onto the heads of the mortified guests!

Escapades such as these almost make a piker out of Aristotle Onassis who, once, with his guests, actors Melina Mercouri and Jules Dassin, decided to visit some night clubs in Athens. In the custom of the Russian czars, Onassis and his guests began to dash plates and cups to the floor, smashing them like Cossacks on leave from the Steppes. Really getting into the spirit of the thing, the trio called for all the dishes to be brought from the kitchen, and, when it was all over, every dish in the place had been smashed to smithereens. Onassis paid a paltry $3,000.00 to the owners for his night's enjoyment.

4

The Last Resort

The Vanderbilt's Hot Springs Hideaway

The housekeeper peeped through the cottage window at the sound of the train whistle. A beautifully gowned lady pointed her tiny foot and stepped from the private railroad car. She turned and spoke to the tall man following her, who laughed and set his tall silk hat back on his head.

"They're here!" The housekeeper raced for the hearth and stooped to light the fire. "Go get their breakfasts," she tossed the order over her shoulder. Then, standing, she glanced around nervously, inspecting as she always did when the spa's most important guests were arriving, to make absolutely certain every detail was perfect. The manager of the Homestead, Mr. Sterry, would be furious if he were to receive even one tiny complaint.

The cottage was spotless, the windows shone like polished diamonds, and the sun beamed in over the resort's fabled lawns, green and sprawling under copper beeches. The beds were freshly made, white and fluffy. Yes, she had done a good job; Mrs. Vanderbilt would be pleased.

At the sound of happy laughter and the solicitous voice of Mr. Sterry welcoming the Vanderbilts during one of their sixty visits to this spa, the housekeeper threw open the door, adding her enormous smile to the welcome. The family's private bellhop began carrying in the dozens of bags and trunks and the maid had begun hanging the delicate silk gowns away in the presses almost before Mr. and Mrs. Vanderbilt were halfway into the room.

In accordance with the Homestead's usual practice of speedy service, the waiter rushed through the door, bearing an enormous silver tray covered with the whitest linen, glancing sunlight off like the dream of some Madison Avenue soap salesman. With a deferential smile, he set the tray on the waiting dining table and whisked off the linen.

Mr. Neily Vanderbilt set to his breakfast with gusto, savoring the country eggs fried to the most delicate turn, their edges just barely crisp and brown, the yolk still liquid gold, and accompanied with generous slices of Smithfield ham cooked in champagne. The Southern biscuits, crusty on the outside and flaky soft on the inside, held a pool of melting butter, freshly churned, awaiting Mr. Vanderbilt's choice of spicy apple butter or sweet orange marmalade. A huge plate of cinnamon rolls, still too hot to touch, oozed brown sugar and butter, lavishly crowned with fresh whole pecan halves glistening in their sugary coat. To freshen a too sweet palate, a bowl of mountain strawberries, garnet red and juicy, sat beside a pitcher of sweet clotted cream. Mrs. Vanderbilt, as was her usual habit, nibbled only on a Spartan breakfast of toast and hot English tea, smiling across the table at her husband enjoying himself.

Family tradition always remarked upon Grace Vanderbilt's marked change in personality upon her arrival at this lovely vacation resort. Tensions of high society entertaining melted away, worries of derrogatory newspaper articles and the cares of living in a public fishbowl drained from her features and she began to relax, becoming childlike again in the fresh air and tree-lined country roads.

After breakfast, it was Grace and Neily's habit to walk, hand in hand, down to the mineral baths, to be separated by custom, Neily heading for the gentlemen's baths and Grace for the ladies'. Enclosed in a soft, muslin granny gown, Grace would step into the steaming mineral baths, partitioned for her privacy, soaking away all the knots of her tense body. One can almost see her, sinking down into the Victorian version of the hot tub, a serene smile creeping across her face. The ever-present maid would quietly wrap her face, now streaming with perspiration, in icy Turkish towels.

Eventually, Mrs. Vanderbilt would climb into a cold shower and, somewhat later still, submit her body to the experienced hands of a masseuse. For over an hour, she would lie there, eyes closed, supremely happy, while the massage continued, first the muscles of the neck, then shoulders becoming relaxed and limp.

On down the body the masseuse worked, her fingers pressing little circles around the muscles on either side of the spine, then drawing the stiffness and strain from Mrs. Vanderbilt's arms, down through the wrists and out through the ends of her dainty fingers.

Finally, the feet. The masseuse stretched the achilles' tendon, rubbing it gently to accustom Mrs. Vanderbilt to the presence of her hands on ultra-sensitive feet. Slowly, very slowly, her hands worked to the sole, rubbing with strong thumbs the tired arches, then pulling the toes forward in a stretching motion.

In ever gentler touches, the masseuse finally ceased her ministration altogether, drawing a linen sheet over Mrs. Vanderbilt's now completely relaxed form, and leaving her to dream in utter serenity.

Meanwhile, across the lawns in the men's baths, Neily would be bathing in the nude, in his own private cubicle, perhaps puffing on an expensive cheroot, and stretching forth his hand to intercept the cork tray floating out to him bearing the tallest, iciest mint julep the South had to offer.

Afternoons were taken up together, Neily and Grace roaming the manicured lawns like two lovers on honeymoon. One looking on might have seen them strolling among the mists of the mineral pools, staring at the creamy white and ruby of the flowering dogwood, blazing away on the slopes of the Alleghenies.

Sometimes, according to family legend, the

couple enjoyed carriage rides, driven by their own personal coachman, leisurely rolling along the Valley Road, gazing at ancient orchards, flowering pink and white and wafting the sweet scents downwind on the breeze. The mountain road curled up and down, sometimes seeming to close in over the country lane with the sheltering limbs of mountain laurel.

The rides were quiet times, Neily sometimes seeming to fall asleep in the warm afternoon sun. It was a time of reverie, serene moments of personal thoughts and pastoral beauty.

Evenings were reserved for entertaining friends, often with those enormous eight or ten course meals so popular at the turn of the century. Conversation sparkled, discussing the latest art works acquired, or perhaps a new musical composition recently heard at recital by a gifted musician. Silent waiters served generous portions of roast wild turkey stuffed with oyster and chestnut dressing, or perhaps a trout caught that afternoon in one of the icy mountain streams and baked to a flaky turn by the talented chefs of the Homestead's kitchens. Other Southern dishes followed, more biscuits, sometimes corn fritters, delicate and light, the golden crust concealing the flaky center.

Away from this gentle Virginia spa, we come to rowdier good times in the wild West. Spencer Penrose, (or Spec, as everyone called him,) one of the copper kings of Utah, was reported to have enjoyed riding up the steps of the fabled Antlers resort hotel on a spirited steed. The proprietors of the Antlers were understandably miffed, some say, when Spec took to shooting drinks out of the hands of startled patrons with his six gun, and thereby banished him forever from their hallowed halls.

Okay, if that was the way they were going to be, Spec would build his own luxury retreat right at the bottom of Cheyenne Mountain, and whisk away the manager and chef of this newly created rival. Spec Penrose's extravagant Broadmoor Hotel opened in 1918, filled with such exotica as only Spec could imagine. He built special ponds about the hotel, importing dozens of seals to stock them. Much to his chagrin, the seals soon discovered they preferred the velvet and potted-palm-filled lobby where they could play with the indulgent guests, who petted the little creatures as though they truly belonged inside a three million dollar luxury hotel. Of course, the water splashed all over the rosewood and oak furniture was not appreciated by Spec Penrose, and soon the seals were on their way back to wherever it is seals come from.

What next? What could Spec bring in to astonish and delight his sometimes jaded guests? Hmmm. Flamingos? Yes, that was a great idea. One can almost imagine Spec Penrose nodding in satisfaction. Flamingos in the middle of Colorado would certainly be a novelty.

Soon the bright pink birds were splashing about in the waters so recently vacated by the ill-fated seals. But it turned out that the flamingos had no better manners than the seals. Who wants to wade around knee-deep in cold water when there are people around? And entrancing smells coming from the dining room?

The chronicles of the Broadmoor Hotel report that, in the middle of some scintillating conversation between ultra-rich ladies and their cigar-smoking mates, and just as a mouthful of succulent broiled trout was about to disappear into a lady's mouth, a bright pink, garish beak would appear just over her shoulder, hell-bent on pecking away at the delicacy on her plate.

Justifiably startled, the lady would screech and throw up her hands, often dumping what was left of her meal all over the oriental carpets. Fleeing in terror, the lady never once looked behind to see her flamingo friend calmly pecking up the remains and gobbling them down with great relish! Alas, the flamingos soon went the way of the seals.

Mr. Penrose scratched his head and thought. Surely *something* extraordinary could be discovered which would not insist on fraternizing with the guests. Spec's imaginative mind again shifted into low gear.

Aha! A skating rink. Perfect. In those days prior to refrigerated hockey and Ice Capade arenas, Spec's mammoth ice rink in the middle of a Colorado July must have been really impressive, even to his ultra-rich guests who thought they'd seen everything.

Spec Penrose loved parties and went to extreme lengths to give Broadmoor guests the most unusual vacations possible. Once, he ordered a whole railroad car of Georgia watermelons shipped in just at their peak, and stored them away in a vast ice house until the middle of January when everybody was thoroughly bored by the wintry blasts of Colorado weather.

Drawing forth the melons, he threw a bash for his guests, serving enormous slices of the red juicy watermelons. Dressed in white dimity and carrying parasols to shade their skin from the non-existent sun, society ladies joined their husbands in the time-honored ritual of eating from point to rind, only taking time to daintily spit out the slick black seeds. Summertime had returned. Apparently it didn't bother Spec in the least that each and every *slice* of melon had cost him nearly $10.00 in pre-inflationary green stuff.

Spec Penrose's main rival, the Antlers, that famed resort hotel, stood as an elegant symbol of the good life to Coloradans until its closing in 1964. What it lacked in Spec's sometimes bizarre grandiose imagination was amply compensated by an incredible luxury, a veritable enactment of old European grace and charm. The towers, with their red tile roofs and tiny balconies, might have been transported from the Borgia's Italian Renaissance. One might have half-expected to see a Florentine lady, dressed in flowing sleeves and pearled caplet, wandering about the gardens during the mists of midnight.

A guest, weary after his long trip from a financial center of the world, could stroll down to a sunroom decorated with all the Oriental opulence of Taj Mahal. Diners basked in deeply padded armchairs covered in glove-soft Spanish leather, their personal elegance reflected in the crystal and mirrors paneling the walls.

Evenings could be spent in a ballroom royally decorated in colors of the most brilliant scarlet and softest ivory, whirling about to the strains of the latest orchestra playing Strauss "Tales from the Vienna Woods."

During the day, after one of the heavy meals of the era, guests could saunter out to a stable filled, not only with blooded horses, but new-fangled bicycles, and wheel themselves down the biking trails thoughtfully laid out by the establishment.

All in all, the Antler's hotel was the quintessential example of Victorian elegance, heavy with Gobelin tapestries and imported English wallpaper, crystal chandeliers and marble statues draped in flowing chitons.

Out on the west coast, in 1879, railroad magnates Hopkins, Crocker, Stanford and Huntington discovered the Monterey Peninsula. Enamored with the area's heroic Wagnerian beauty, the men purchased almost all the California peninsula's vacant land, building shortly thereafter the Hotel Del Monte, a Victorian resort rivaling the Colorado Springs Antler's for opulence.

But, by the 1920's, the tastes of the super-rich had changed. Victorian velvets and gingerbread were too heavy for this new era. In 1919, Samuel Morse, grandnephew to the telegraph's inventor, bought the property from the quartet. Morse, enthralled too with the natural beauty of the rugged coastline, envisioned a resort built around the natural state of things.

Thousands of acres of coastline were left exactly the way wind and waves created them. Adventurous guests were left free to wander the jagged outcroppings, etched away by the breakers into a piece of an impossibly difficult jigsaw puzzle. They saw the land just as Robert Louis Stevenson had seen it as he gathered inspiration for *Treasure Island*, describing the "great rollers, thundering and thundering by day and night." Cypresses, gnarled and twisted by the everlasting winds blowing off the Pacific Ocean, guarded the headlands and the legendary road which was eventually to become known as Seventeen Mile Drive, home of fabulous mansions necklacing the coastline.

To be sure, Morse provided a racetrack, polo fields and bridle paths for wealthy horse lovers, as well as tennis courts for the athletic, and even a trapshooting range for clay pigeon sharp-shooters. But perhaps his most incredible achievements were the five golf courses, including Cypress Point Club and Pebble Beach, incredibly difficult championship courses, even today played on by Jack Nicklaus and Andy Bean in the U.S. Open and the Bing Crosby Pro-Amateur Tournaments. These monumental links, man-made only because Morse laid them out in opposition to the rocky crags of the coastline, gave wealthy golfers the added challenges of battling off-shore winds, jagged boulders, and salt spray.

The area is so incredibly beautiful, however, that man can do nothing to improve it. Wealthy guests of the Del Monte Resort, if jaded at the splendor of man-shaped gold and gems, could still be startled and delighted as a child when coming upon, unexpectedly, a whole tree upholstered in Monarch butterflies, shimmering in the breeze like a bouquet of black-tinged marigolds. California sea lions barked hoarsely down the coastline, startling wealthy intruders, the gentle creatures warning curious humans away. Huge fields of artichokes bloomed like thistly flowers, waiting to prick the finger of an unwary gourmet, or to grace his table bathed in clarified lemon butter.

For spiritually-minded millionaries, a trip to Father Junipero Serra's Spanish Mission at Carmel was a must, certainly not for the buildings, for in the 1920's and 1930's before restoration, many of the structures were in ruins. But, ruins or not, the peace of such a holy place, used for prayer since 1771, remained a tangible thing. One seems able to hear God's Voice ever more clearly in places such as these.

But, as Robert Louis Stevenson said a century ago, "the one common note of all this country is the haunting presence of the ocean."

It would be a world-weary millionaire indeed who could not spend endless entranced hours gazing into the mists above a coast bombarded with crashing waves. Whether overhung by sunshine or fog, the colors of the ocean, ever-changing, ever-fascinating, shimmer like light caught precariously in God's prism. Seagulls dive and swoop above the waves with serious intensity, like Jonathan Livingston desperately trying to figure out how to get from here to there in an instant. Cormorants sail low above the water, waiting to scoop down in a flat

Olympic racer's dive, guzzling up some delicacy of the sea.

And always, always, the eternal pounding of the surf, a hypnotic accompaniment to reverie, a thundering counterpoint to philosophical musings. A place to feel either very, very small, or, at one with the magnificence of God's universe, a place to feel very, very large.

5

Wedding Veils and Vagabonds

The Fairy Tale Wedding of Monte Carlo

Washington, D.C., was in a dither. Congress was having a hard time keeping its mind on running the country. Highly placed dignitaries from foreign governments all over the world had been arriving for weeks bearing gifts of incredible opulence. And, though it was cold that February in 1906, the warmth and excitement of Valentine's week completely obliterated any discomfort. "Princess" Alice Roosevelt was to be wed to the dashing Congressman from Ohio, Nicholas Longworth, and romance was the order of the day. For weeks, no one had talked about anything else.

Alice Roosevelt had attained star quality. Her pre-wedding parties and shopping trips for trousseau commanded front page columns in newspapers, and outgoing, irrepressible Alice was rather enjoing it all. Her bedroom in the White House, along with the rest of the entire top floor, was awash in gifts. In addition to the showers of presents from American nabobs and common folks, "small tokens" kept arriving from overseas.

Couriers from both King Alfonso of Spain and the German Kaiser arrived bearing heavy antique jewelry to grace Alice's arms; good Pope Pius X sent a beautiful mosaic from the Vatican. King Edward dispatched an enameled snuffbox as a gift from the people of England, and the King of Italy shipped a mosaic table from Florence so heavy it could never be used in any ordinary home. From fabled Japan, the Mikado transmitted a brace of silver vases and rolls upon rolls of precious silk, and, from France, the President's emissary hand-carried a "priceless" Gobelin tapestry woven especially for the Roosevelt-Longworth wedding and appraised at $25,000.00 in 1906 currency. Another gift reportedly worth $25,000.00 was an incredible pearl and diamond necklace from the government of Cuba.

Stepping over and around mounds of jewelry, tea sets, plates, candleholders and vases, Alice surveyed her dowry. Someone called her attention to a new gift just arriving. Carefully carrying a beautiful teak chest into the room, aides announced that it was from the Empress Dowager of China. The family is reported to have halted everything to examine this new treasure. From dozens of compartments, Alice drew forth wonders—rolls of brocaded silk from one; an ermine coat from another, floating white and feathery; a fox coat from yet another, its rich deep sable color contrasting sharply with the snowy ermine; another compartment gave up ancient Chinese carvings. Alice was entranced. "The Chinese," she is reported to have commented, "had a very proper idea of gifts."

A delegation of Ponca Indians, fearful that all this attention to the bride might emasculate her groom, arrived from Oklahoma to present Nicholas with a buffalo skin vest. And, one perfectly charming little old lady, probably virtually penniless, nevertheless sent her love along with a paper of pins.

The morning of February 17th, crowds of excited Americans grouped about the White House, anxious for even one glimpse of the festivities or for a sight of those favored invitees who would enjoy the wedding close up. Carriages and diplomatic motor cars began to arrive late in the morning, the wealthy and powerful occupants excited to be among the few invited guests and anxious to get into the White House first and get a good seat.

An entire nation held its breath as the time ball descended on the White House roof, like Times Square on New Year's Eve. The crystal drops of the chandeliers in the East Room shimmered over guests arrayed in diamonds and silks. Gold damask draperies accented the gold trim on the newly painted walls. A room so often used for affairs of state was completely transformed into a garden bower of white and American Beauty roses, rhododendron in pale tints of pink and white, with swooping ropes of smilax.

There, in front of the east window where the marriage was to take place, had been placed a dais, now covered with a rich Oriental carpet.

Framing the dais and the east window was a glistening gold cloth, magically transfiguring a simple window into an altar of God, with brilliant white and gold Easter lilies forming a sunburst at its center.

Suddenly, the strains of *Lohengrin* rang out from the Marine orchestra and the guests craned their necks for a glimpse of the bride. Alice, poised elegantly on the arm of her father, President Teddy Roosevelt, entered through an honor guard of military aides, their uniforms resplendent. Some of the guests were surprised to see that there were no bridesmaids, but Alice had earlier shrugged them off in her forthright manner. All her friends were married now and unsuitable for bridesmaids, and, anyway, she had always thought bridal processions "peculiar." So *that* took care of *that*.

Alice was said to have been such a beautiful bride that she took the breath away. Her heavy satin wedding gown enhanced her wasp waist, and the long cathedral train whispered down the carpet behind her. Alice's dark hair, brushed and shining, was swept up into an elegant Gibson Girl pompadour and covered with a coronet of orange blossoms, trailing a wispy veil. Trimming the satin gown was exquisite rose-point lace which had adorned both her grandmother's and her mother's wedding dresses.

Alice and her father, the President, stepped up to the dais and, with a dazzling smile, she held out her hand to Nicholas, dressed in a dove grey frock coat, with a moonstone in his tie for good luck. And, with the February sunshine flooding in, the two were wed.

Later, after most of the guests of state were gone, the close friends (some of whom included the fabulously wealthy Grace Wilson Vanderbilt and the Goelets) attended a wedding breakfast, enjoying such delicacies as hothouse fruits, salads, petit fours decorated with swirls of pastel icing, ice cream shaped into little hearts, and sandwiches of every kind and description. Champagne flowed into the guests' glasses in endless waterfalls.

Presented with the sword of a White House Marine, Alice sliced the wedding cake to the cheers of the guests. Shortly, someone arrived bearing a gift of a tiny Manchurian puppy, which the ever-enthusiastic Alice squeezed in delight.

The whole country rejoiced. Babies arriving that day and for weeks afterward were christened "Alice." It was some time before the government got back down to the business of running a country. In 1906, things were simpler.

Another presidential wedding took place between Ethel DuPont and Franklin D. Roosevelt, Jr. In a gallant courtship from the hallowed halls of Harvard, the young Roosevelt was reported to once have smashed a reporter's camera who attempted to take a picture his Ethel did not want, and later, after Ethel had been away on a jaunt to Europe, hired a plane to fly out and welcome her home. It seemed inevitable that another wedding between power and money take place.

Late in June of 1937, with Hitler's faithful

singing the Horst Wessel in Germany, all was still roses and orange blossoms in the Delaware home of the DuPonts'. The enormous family was stuffed into a tiny church, and, with young Roosevelt standing at the railing and President Franklin Delano Roosevelt looking on, Ethel and her attendants began down the aisle. Dressed in white tulle, bride and bridesmaids looked like something from a Bolshoi presentation of *Swan Lake*, the effect of shimmering clouds broken only by the pale lavender and blue in their bouquets.

Ethel's gown was sprinkled with fresh orange blossoms, encircling her waist and dotting the Juliet cap on her head. Caught from the headpiece was a feathery veil which floated out behind her for twelve feet.

In a privately amusing departure from ceremony, the minister omitted the words "with all my wordly goods I thee endow" from the vows which young Franklin Roosevelt spoke. When one marries a DuPont, it does not seem to be necessary.

In a bethrothal which shocked the world, Aristotle Onassis took the hand of the widow of fallen president, John Fitzgerald Kennedy. Inside a tiny chapel on the private island of Skorpios on October 20, 1968, Jacqueline Bouvier Kennedy, in an eggshell lace dress by Valentino, and the old Greek shipmaster, dressed in a baggy double-breasted suit of navy blue, clasped their hands before the sight of only twenty-two family witnesses. With the fresh smell of a light shower falling outside mingling with the sweet perfume of gardenias, a Greek Orthodox priest appeared in his traditional high black hat, square black beard, and golden vestments to solemnly intone the traditional Greek vows. Artemis, the groom's sister, placed wreaths of white ribbons and lemon flowers on their heads as the simple gold bands were passed back and forth three times, symbolizing the Christian Trinity.

After kissing a silver goblet of wine and drinking together, Jackie and Ari followed the priest three times around the altar in the Dance of Esiah and soon the wedding was over.

Arms folded and feet spread apart, a U.S. Secret Service man barred the door to outsiders, moving aside only as the couple came toward him, the P.T.-109 tie clip glittering in the twilight in an ironic touch.

What the wedding had espoused in simplicity was more than made up for in the crush of publicity and reporters. Outside the chapel, all was pandemonium. Flashbulbs exploded, but *only* when Onassis said so. No expense was spared to protect the island's privacy. Private patrol boats and helicopters with electronic bullhorns policed the perimeter of the island, beefed up with additional helicopters and ships from nothing less than the Greek Navy.

Finally slipping away from the gaggle of journalists, the couple and their family sped away to the ultimate luxury and privacy of the beautiful yacht. *Christina,* to begin their singularly non-private life together.

If Onassis' wedding was simplicity itself,

there was another wedding in which he himself contributed in good measure to the decidedly carnival atmosphere.

In 1956, the storybook wedding between America's Golden Girl, Grace Kelly, and Prince Ranier III seized the imagination of the world. It seemed too good to be true, like something straight out of Grimm's Fairy Tales, the beautiful commoner swept away by the handsome prince to live happily ever after.

The Cathedral of St. Nicholas was redolent with the luscious scent and graceful curves of white lilacs, drooping even from golden baskets hanging from high chandeliers. The bride, dressed in Brussels lace studded with tiny pearls, gazed up at her groom, the prince resplendent in his Monogasque uniform laden with medals and gold braid. The newspapers say the princess spoke with a trembling voice, misty-eyed, adding to the fairy-tale legend of the affair.

Swooping down the aisle after the vows, the royal couple ascended into their open-carriaged Rolls-Royce, parading through the streets of Monaco to wildly cheering throngs.

Finally arriving at a tiny chapel under Monte Carlo's railroad bridge, the new Princess Grace knelt in the dirt, oblivious to her lace hem, and prayed to the patron saint of Monaco, St. Devote, to bless their new marriage. After kissing the relics of the Saint offered by the black-robed priests, the bride laid her wedding flowers at the statue of this Saint who had been responsible for bringing Christianity to their land.

Cannons boomed as the couple was aided back into the Rolls-Royce to continue the tour of the city, and the fireworks began, cascading down upon the city thousands of little Monagasque flags from tiny parachutes.

About this time, according to reports, the noise of a seaplane was heard overheard. Looking up, the citizens could see the markings of Aristotle Onassis on its side as, suddenly, thousands upon thousands of red and white carnations showered from the sky, falling upon the happy wedding couple and their ecstatic subjects.

In addition to the carnation cascade, Onassis, to show his devotion to his friend, gave the bride an exquisite diamond necklace, as well as donating one million francs to one of the Prince's favorite charities. It was a most satisfactory wedding gift.

Six years later, not too far away in southwestern France, another marriage was taking place. This was a very different princess, a beautiful young woman with roots of wealth and power stretching back into the eighteenth century. With almost two centuries of incredible riches behind her, the wedding was the zenith of the quiet elegance of aristocracy, although the citizens of the village waited to cheer her wedding party with as much enthusiasm as for the storybook Ranier's.

Shiny black limousines moved slowly through the streets, looking for all the world like a high diplomatic motorcade, although the first car was completely blanketed in orchids from

Edmund de Rothschild's teak greenhouses.

Inside the orchid-banked Rolls-Royce, Philippine Rothschild waited, dressed in a deceptively simple white satin Balenciaga gown. Her veil was securely clasped in place by a coronet of white mink, ornamented by stars of diamonds.

Just before she entered the chapel, a maid handed her a simple spray of fragrant apple blossoms, flown in specially that morning all the way from Turkey.

At the reception, high society guests admired a wedding cake almost seven feet tall. At its top, recreated in spun sugar, were the five arrows celebrated in the Rothschild family crest—no cupids allowed here. And, in place of the inevitable wedding photographer, the family had flown in, straight from Buckingham Palace, Sir Cecil Beaton, who photographed the affair dressed in top hat and morning coat.

The guests, too, were handsomely cared for. Private Pullman cars had been chartered to bring them all the way from Paris, and, on board, the famous hairdresser of the super-rich, Alexandre, waited to style an errant curl. Champagne and caviar were served in pipeline abundance by butlers whose only task was to see to every comfort of the Rothschild guests.

Two of the United State's Irish rich families were united with the marriage of Joseph B. Murray and Theresa Farrell. Like the Rothschilds, they chartered an entire train to bring wedding guests from Grand Central Station to Connecticut. And, like Alice

Roosevelt Longworth's gifts cluttering up the White House, the Farrell-Murray gifts stacked up and overflowed in the Farrell mansion.

After a beautiful wedding, the party retired to the garden for the traditional champagne and wedding cake. Before their horrified eyes, flames shot up through the roof of the mansion. The whole house seemed to explode.

Men attempted to force their way into the house to save thousands and thousands of dollars of wedding gifts, but, when the walls began to sway, the bride's father barred the way, refusing to allow anyone to attempt it. "Don't worry," he is reported to have told them, "It's all insured."

Another Irish wedding which ended on a happier note was between Henry Ford and Anne McDonnell, who had once been engaged to John F. Kennedy. Members of the Ford family arrived from all over the world. Edsel Ford and his family sailed in on their private yacht, the *Onika*, and anchored in the bay at Southampton. Other guests, equally important, arrived the day of the wedding; John F. Kennedy himself was joined by dozens of Catholic priests and bishops.

After the vows, solemnly pronounced by the-then-Monsignor Fulton J. Sheen, Henry Ford, Sr., held out his hand to his granddaughter-in-law and danced on the lawn at the McDonnell mansion, to the lilting strains of Strauss' waltz, "The Voices of Spring."

Another marriage filled with luminaries was the wedding of Sharon Percy, daughter of Senator Charles Percy from Illinois, and Jay Rockefeller.

Lynda Bird Johnson showed up on the arm of actor George Hamilton at a time when the two were "an item." Maurice Chevalier, the famous French actor famous for singing "Thank Heaven for Little Girls," arrived, in respect for many years of friendship with the Percy family.

Rockefellers lined the front pews of the Cathedral, and, with all the other political powers there, it looked like a national convention, as Gov. and Mrs. George Romney of Michigan sat side by side with Mayor and Mrs. John V. Lindsay of New York.

But the day belonged to the bride and groom, their handsome and happy faces beaming forth the joy they so obviously felt. Flowers crowded the sanctuary, from Sharon's beautiful and unusual cream-colored rhododendron-and-roses bouquet to the tiny sprig of lilies-of-the-valley on Jay's lapel.

In contrast to the Spartan simplicity of Jackie and Aristotle Onassis' ceremony, Jay and Sharon's entrance was preceded by no fewer than nine bridesmaids wearing coronets of fresh flowers, one tiny blonde flower girl, and a ring-bearer in lace collar and cuffs, knee breeches, and polished buckled pumps.

If modern weddings tend to revolve around flowers, the Astor's preferred diamonds. When Ava Willing married John Jacob Astor IV, her immense veil was secured by an incredible diamond tiara, a gift from her groom. And, at her throat, in lieu of the modern traditional strand of pearls, lay a gift from her future mother-in-law, a diamond lover's knot, as big as her hand. And, instead of the more common white tulle and peau de soie, the future Mrs. Astor donned a gown of silver made by the famous dressmakers to the super-rich, Worth of Paris.

For many newlyweds, honeymoons consist of a night in a local motel, before returning to work on Monday. There is none of that among the super-rich.

Sharon and Jay Rockefeller flew off to the Orient, luxuriating in the serenity of Japanese gardens in which gravel is swirled about in careful waves to simulate the movement of the sea. Henry and Anne Ford took off for the tropical paradise of early 1940's Hawaii, lolling about on the creamy beaches and drinking fresh pineapple punches with flowers floating in the glass. And Alice and Nicholas Longworth spent their honeymoon in a Cuba that people of the 1980's cannot imagine. At the turn of the century, Cuba was truly an Eden, warm and sunny, and the rich were served with a deference that our more egalitarian age will probably never know.

When Ned Green finally married after the death of his mother, he decided on his dream honeymoon, floating about on the biggest yacht in the world. Unfortunately, he married during United States' wartime, and all the ships of the size he desired had been pressed into service. Finally finding a passenger boat about the size he had in mind, he bought it and had the entire thing *cut in half* and forty extra feet added. Fitting it with monumental luxury, Green and his bride made ready to sail. But before the voyage could be launched, the unfortunate vessel sank in its harbor. Green had to be satisifed with a smaller ship, one that slept a mere seventy persons, and he sailed away, disgruntled, with his bride.

Aristotle Onassis already *had* his dream yacht. After the wedding of Jackie and Ari, they slipped away to the privacy of its opulence. Here no more paparazzi could reach them, no more screaming reporters could jar the perfection of these first days, no prying eyes and judgmental tongues, berating the president's widow for what was perceived by many as her double-cross.

Perhaps in the still of the gathering dusk, by the light of flickering candles, Jackie may have entertained her new husband by playing a Chopin etude on the yacht's grand piano.

After a time of solitude, the servants would have brought in the supper meal, served in sterling silver dishes. All the food treasures of Greece might have been served. Perhaps there was a plate of *beccafica*, whose tiny birds pickled in vinegar which are meant to be eaten with the fingers, bones and all, a gourmet's delicacy from the island of Cyprus. Breads there would have been in abundance, crusty and warm. In the center of the table may have been a giant silver tray of fresh frits, figs and grapes, watermelon, juicy and succulent, and almonds and chestnuts. Cheeses to go along with the fruit would certainly have been offered, as well as the plump black olives of Skorpios. Along with the rest might have come a platter of lamb, baked to perfection in grape leaves, and, to finish the meal, baklava and other sweet pastries.

After they had eaten their fill, Ari may have opened a favorite bottle of Dom Perignon, the beverage he had so often in earlier years shared with his friend, Winston Churchill. But tonight his friend was his wife, and they must have toasted themselves with secret smiles, luxuriating in the warmth of the flames in the fireplace, and enjoyed the private happiness of these first moments together.

Nelson Rockefeller did not need to be concerned with the crush of reporters and photographers as did Onassis. He and his wife, Mary Todhunter Clark Rockefeller, were free to embark upon an excursion few would ever see. Rockefeller power and wealth opened unimaginable doors to the young couple. They needn't worry about traveling with a tour guide, or trying to find places of interest on their own. Wherever the newlyweds traveled, an enthusiastic representative of the Rockefeller empire took them in hand, escorting them to special sights and experiences only a local might know, and setting up interviews with dignitaries and heads of state.

Throughout the Pacific, the young couple toured. In Hawaii, they may have been shown the beauty of some secret island sanctuary, with flaming St. Johnianus hibiscus or a rare "yellow-thighed oo," or the cloud-banked slopes of Waialeale, its icy cataracts pulsing down moutainsides blanketed with yam vines. Perhaps they were taken to see Kalalau Valley, where oddly-shaped cones were carved by erosion, then covered with rain-forest green.

Traveling on to legendary Japan, Nelson and Mary Rockefeller would have been met by a new set of Standard Oil hosts. Perhaps knowing the Rockefeller passion for creative excellence, they may have been taken to visit Japanese artists creating the finest lacquered cranes of conch shell, shaved paper thin, and of quail eggshells, ground into the finest powder; or to a dollmaker, carving exquisite figures of the finest Paulownia wood and garbing them in fabrics woven and dyed by the artist. Perhaps they may have visited a swordsmith, forging an ornate *tachi*, the Samurai sword, of beaten steel, or seen the stylized beauty of the best Kabuki theatre.

Rockefeller would have loved the *shibui*, or restrained elegance, of the Japanese temples, rising in gentle swooping curves, and the more ornate gilded buddhas, expressing serenity in every line. Perhaps the newlyweds were taken to the finest eating places for a meal of *sushi* and steamed fluffy rice, accompanied with rounded cakes of *mochi*.

Later, on the remote island of Bali, the company representatives might have treated Nelson and Mary to the Ketchak dance, the ancient story of the Ramayana, with over a hundred dancers, most portraying the famous monkeys. And, later, they may have partaken of luscious Balinese food to the sound of gamelon music.

In Bangkok, the city of the angels, they may

have seen more of the exotic buddhas, some golden, like the famous Reclining Buddha, some with pottery bodies covered with thousands of colorful porcelain chips.

And, in India, they may have been treated to elephant rides, their mahout colorfully turbanned and uniformed in scarlet, the elephant itself carrying a howdah of embroidered gold.

They may have visited the beautiful stone trelliswork of Jaipur's Palace of the Winds, where once the maharajah's ladies peeked out at the world, or seen the marble palace of Udaipur, appearing to float on the waters of Lake Pichola. And even a Rockefeller would have to make the traditional trip to the Taj Mahal, which many believe to be the most beautiful tomb in the world, erected by the Shah Jehan when his beloved Mumtaz died.

But in addition to all these sights and sounds and scents in the exotic places, doors were opened to the highest government officials, such as the Viceroy of India.

Traveling to Delhi, the couple visited with the great Indian poet, Tagore, and, then, in the apex of anyone's honeymoon, they went to the home of Mahatma Gandhi. Rockefeller himself wrote about this momentous meeting, telling that when the couple first arrived, the "Great Soul" was having one of his days of silence, but, in a gesture of hospitality, he passed the couple a slip of paper, inviting them to return the next day.

At five o'clock in the morning, the Rockefellers rolled up to the old ascetic's house.

Speaking without restriction this time, Gandhi told the Rockefellers all about his difficult life as an Indian lawyer in England and in South Africa, and how he developed his philosophy of non-violent resistance to the British colonial policy towards India, pointing toward the great influence of the essay, *Civil Disobedience,* written by Rockefeller's countryman, Henry David Thoreau. Rockefeller reports that he was enthralled with the visit, having learned so much about Gandhi and the Indian point of view. It was to be an event that even the super-rich Rockefeller treasured for the rest of his life.

6

Toy Boats

Onassis' Floating Palace

The bright June morning was exciting and full of promise. On deck, the crew polished imaginary dust specks off already gleaming brass fittings. On shore, ten sailors sporting natty blue uniforms with trim of spotless white inspected each other, holding up the brass buttons to their lips to breathe on, then polish with their sleeves. One of them continually stared into the distance, his ear cocked for the first keening whistle of the locomotive. The air crackeled with excitement. Today was to be the maiden voyage of the new yacht!

At the first sound of the private train, the crewmen snapped to attention, trying to peer upward for the first glimpse of the Gould clan while retaining their stiff naval posture.

On board the private railroad car filled with rich velvets and rocking chairs of wicker, the Gould's were as enthusiastic as the crewmen. Jay Gould had issued strict instructions to the ship-builders. This was to be the finest vessel ever built, the grandest, the most luxurious. And, from tales floating back from the shipyards, they had succeeded.

The Gould's hurried to the dock as quickly as their dignified status would allow. The first sight of the vessel was breathaking. Riding easily in the water, her masts swept back as if perpetually in flight and her spear-like prow piercing the waves ahead, the *Atalanta* looked as sleek as the Greek lady for whom she was named, that legendary goddess who refused all suitors who could not outrun her.

The family was assisted into the cutter by the ten sailors, and, soon, the oars began to dip and pulse into the waves of the harbor. Upon arrival at the sleek and elegant *Atalanta*, they were piped aboard with all the exaggerated ceremony and aplomb of a Gilbert and Sullivan operetta.

The next wonderful hours were spent in exploring the family's new treasure, like children with an incredible Christmas toy. The whole ship was built and decorated in something called American Renaissance, which was merely a Victorian style taken to its ultimate gingerbread. The walls were paneled in the rarest woods, mahogany and rosewood. The floors, hiding under Oriental rugs of deep wine colors, were parqueted in hardwoods, colors and grains of sycamore, red cedar, California laurel, swirly butternut, and maple gleaming in pleasing variety.

Richly upholstered furniture filled the salons, covered in silk damasks and crimson velvets. Gold monogrammed velvet draperies blanketed the walls. In the yacht library, gold-stamped leather volumes were fastened in their rosewood shelves with leather bands to keep them from falling out on rough high seas. Also securely fastened in place was the built-in baby grand piano, along with all the crystal and porcelain carefully selected and brought aboard to make the house a home.

Down in Jay Gould's own cabin, silk draperies shot through with silver and gold threads covered the paneled walls. And, in this day of no running water, his bathroom held an incredible luxury—a sunken tub of marble.

The ship's innards were fitted with the most up-to-date devices of 1883. Down in the hold chugged ice machines, pumping out ice cubes for the family's beverages, the latest design pilfered from the U.S. Navy, and, throughout the yacht, Thomas Alva Edison's freshly-patented light bulbs flickered. In the galley, three French chefs already labored in the gourmet kitchens, preparing the sumptuous lunch for the Gould family and guests. More important than the three French cooks was the special Viennese pastry chef, piping out his crusty, melting ladyfingers, the staple of Jay Gould's diet.

How much did it cost to run a floating pleasure dome like the *Atalanta*? As J. P. Morgan once said in his famous quote, "Nobody who has to ask what a yacht costs has any business owning one." But it is reported that the *Atalanta* cost Jay Gould $10,000 per week to maintain. And, in today's soft-edged, float-to-the-ceiling currency, that translates to over one quarter of a million dollars . . . *per week!*

In those days of the Gould's and the Morgan's and the Vanderbilt's greatest wealth, each new yacht strove to outdo the last. Individual quirks were accommodated.

When J. P. Morgan decided to build Corsair III, his third yacht, he decided it should be bigger than the other two, but that the interior fittings must be exactly the same as Corsair II. Now this might cause a set-back, he was told, as the carpets originally installed in Corsair II were no longer being made. But to J. P. Morgan and his millions, that was no problem at all. He merely instructed the carpet company to set up the old patterns on their present looms and build him the rugs he desired. They did.

On Vincent Astor's *Nourmahal*, a magnificent dining hall richly walled in black walnut ran the entire *length* of the yacht, over 250 feet long.

When our old friend, James Gordon Bennett, built his *Lysistrata*, complete attention was made for *his* special interests. A set of bedrooms was fitted especially for Bennett's use; no one but Bennett ever slept in these. Below decks, an incredible Turkish bath, complete with steam rooms, exercise equipment, and masseur was built for Bennett's health; no one but Bennett ever used it.

To supply the milk and cream for Bennett's freshly churned butter and his milk punches, an elaborate padded stall was built, and within the confines of this opulent mini-barn, a pampered Alderney cow lived. Whenever the ship sailed through waters of the equator, there was an electric fan to keep old Bossie cool; whenever traveling in northern climates, the finest wool blankets were carefuly draped over her glossy flanks to keep her warm. And, just in case the animal went dry or began to have problems with her milk, alternates were kept standing by, tested for just the right butterfat content, in every port Bennett might want to visit.

Trips with James Gordon Bennett were exciting, to say the least. No one was ever sure how long they would be out, or where they would be going. One time, a troupe of actors was hired to entertain the guests at an afternoon tea party in the harbor, only to find themselves well out to sea at performance's end. The yacht steamed back into port sometime late the next day, with both the troupe and the theatre owner generously paid for their inconvenience.

Not so funny were the times when Bennett sailed away with parties which included wives of other men, bringing them home again the next morning in bedraggled evening gowns, the ultimate indignity. To keep from fighting duels for their honor, or, worse yet, from being horsewhipped himself by an angry husband, Bennett cheerfully sent creamy pearl necklaces and diamond tiaras to the angry women, with formal apologies to their irate spouses.

For Neily Vanderbilt, his yacht *North Star* was a place of retreat, away from the rounds of his wife's endless parties, American Beauty roses, and pink silk damasks. His library was stocked with books he loved, adventure, mostly, which he would read for hours on end to his children. Afternoons were trips into fantasy with Kipling and Robert Louis Stevenson, H. G.

Wells and Sir Arthur Conan Doyle's *Sherlock Holmes*. On storm-lashed days on the high seas, Vanderbilt would curl up with his son and daughter and, in ringing tones, *Twenty Thousand Leagues Under the Sea* would come to life, accompanied by the roaring gales and pounding waves against the side of the yacht.

The *North Star*, by Vanderbilt's own insistence, remained a place for things masculine. Navy blazers with shiny silver buttons were worn by family and crew. Beds were covered in finest Irish linen, embroidered with Vanderbilt's monogram, and over which lay French blankets trimmed in navy silk. The wine cellar was filled with his choices of finest wines and liqueurs, claret and Grand Marnier.

But, in spite of everything, Grace Vanderbilt had to have a finger in the decorating. Rosewood tables often held Imari bowls and tortoise shell cigarette boxes. From time to time, one would stumble across a wicker wastebasket lined with pink silk. One can almost imagine Cornelius Vanderbilt throwing up his hands in an "I give up" attitude, and retreating to his library to smoke his smelly Turkish cigarettes in revenge.

But, if Neily Vanderbilt had to make concessions on his yacht to his wife, Edmond Rothschild did not. The very essence of the ship bespoke Rothschild's heritage. Once, when leaders of the fledgling Jewish settlements in Palestine were invited aboard his vessel for a conference, they were amazed at the cultural treasures. Sitting down to dinner, they were served gourmet meals which also, incidentally, were kosher. Retiring later to their staterooms, they found, attached to the doorposts, mezzuzahs containing the required Scriptures from Deuteronomy. And, coming together later for worship, the elders discovered the satin-lined prayer room was set thoughtfully in the most stable part of the yacht, so prayers would not be disturbed by anything so unpleasant as seasickness.

Rothschild legends tell that when it was time for the elders to return to Palestine, one old gentleman nearly missed the boat. When he was found much later still wandering about the decks gazing in disbelief at the wonders, another elder chided him. In retort, he is supposed to have answered, "You go on to the Promised Land. I'll stay on the Promised Yacht."

But with all the heavy luxury of the Victorian millionaires' yachts, nothing can touch the modern opulence of the *Christina*, Aristotle Onassis' floating home. Although Onassis had insisted upon his own personal quarters on every vessel he owned, he dreamed of the day when he might build a ship totally his own, totally home, totally private, to take him wherever he wanted to go or to escape from wherever he didn't want to be.

Finally, in the early 1950's, Onassis bought a ship for $34,000, and proceeded to spend over four million dollars in steady Eisenhower currency to fit her out in the style in which he had become accustomed.

Completely self-contained, the ship held every convenience modern science had yet devised.

The generator pumped out enough electricity for a city of ten thousand; an electronic control panel in the wheelhouse blinked an insistent red at any open porthole or if the temperature rose above normal anywhere on the ship. The finest radios and ship-to-shore phone system kept Onassis in touch with the world. The story is told that once Onassis boasted that he could reach any place in the world from the *Christina*. Scoffing, a guest did not believe that a phone system limited by water could do so. Picking up the phone, Aristotle dialed the guest's mother in Washington, D.C., and handed him the phone for an unexpected chat.

An advanced stabilizer system was installed to keep the yacht from rolling or pitching in anything but the most violent storms. And, if any other vehicle might be needed in an emergency, the *Christina* kept a stable of seaplanes, Chriscrafts, hydrofoil speedboats, kayaks, *and* a white Fiat onboard which could be deployed at a moment's notice.

The most modern of hospitals was maintained, including an x-ray department and a complete surgery, and in any voyage over one day's length, a doctor traveled in the crew's contingent. This was to be especially important in Onassis' later days as myasthenia gravis pulled his eyelids further and further down, and weakened and drained this vital man.

But, in the early days, jet setters from all over the world reveled in invitations to the luxurious *Christina*. Arriving on board the scrupulously white ship, guests first set foot on a teak deck, varnished and buffed to perfection. All around them polished brass shone in the Mediterranean sunshine.

Arriving at the corridor to their quarters, guarded by two mammoth bronze falcons, guests were treated to their first indication of Onassis' first love, Greece. Each of the doors to the nine guest suites were emblazoned with a gold-leaf plate picturing the shape of a different Greek island, with its name above it in both Greek and English.

The entire ship was enough to make even the wealthiest jet-setters feel poor. Up on deck lay an exquisite mosaic floor, a reproduction of one excavated from ancient Crete. This beautiful mosaic might serve as a dance floor on fresh Aegean evenings, and for dining on sunny days. But, at the push of the multi-millionaire's finger, the floor would begin to descend, further and further, until it became the bottom of a swimming pool, where guests could dive and float like ancient Greeks in marble palaces. And, at night, the pool became a fountain, complete with lights playing over the waters in colors that matched the tiles of the mosaic itself.

Near to the magnificent mosaic floor was the Game Room, a living area much loved by Onassis himself. Entering in through antique Japanese lacquered doors, a guest would find himself in an oak paneled room with heavy beamed ceilings, not at all the kind of thing to expect on a boat. The floors were covered with thick Turkish rugs from Smyrna, and, in the corner, a grand piano waited for talented fingers to bring forth its music. A fireplace studded in lapis lazuli was perpetually set with firewood, ready to be set ablaze to ward off a night chill blowing off the Mediterranean.

A motion picture theatre was provided with all the latest films, to be shown at the pleasure of the shipmaster or his guests. One did not need to wait till showtime; the film ran whenever the *viewers* were ready.

In one salon was a circular bar containing a replica of the sea covered over with glass. Tiny ships played in the blue waters and could be moved about by players with tiny magnets. Everywhere were models of Napoleon's ships, painstakingly carved from creamy ivory by the French Emperor's seamen wasting away in prisons after his defeats.

For meals, guests were treated to further examples of Onassis' love of things Greek. The formal silver was especially designed to look like the utensils used in ancient Crete, and the egg-shell china sported the gold seal of Greece in the center. Baccarat crystal, pinging at a touch, bore the imprint of the *Christina's* flag on its base.

But, upstairs, Onassis' private life could unfold in luxury even more incredible than the rest of the ship. Here in this oaken retreat hung an El Greco painting reportedly worth nearly three million dollars, and, in its own case, sat a ruby-encrusted jade buddha fashioned by the master jeweler of a Russian czar, one of only three in the world, priceless. The bedroom, with walls of soft ivory and a green the color of Onassis' beloved sea, was filled with antique Venetian furniture, ornate, rare woods trimmed in gold. On the walls hung a multitude of Greek icons, those beautiful panels of wood painted with saints and madonnas.

Perhaps the bathroom begins to indicate the depth of Onassis' love for Greek history. An exact replica of ancient King Minos' bath, it held a tub of blue, white and gold mosaics, topped with gold faucets, replicas of those incredible spigots in the legendary Chateau de la Croe from which he was banished at its purchase by his arch-rival, Stavros Niarchos. Switching on the water, Onassis had his choice of hot or cold fresh water, *or* hot or cold salt water for his bath!

Another reader, like Neily Vanderbilt, Onassis filled his library with Greek histories and mythology, including Sir Arthur Evans' scholarly work on the excavation of the Palace of Knossos on Crete.

Onassis, though having gone to the jungles of Brazil to make his initial fortune, was drawn back to his native land as surely as if he had been tethered by a silken cord. Now sailing about the seas of the Mediterranean, the Aegean, and the Ionian on the sumptuous *Christina*, Onassis had the time, the money, and the privacy to enjoy it all.

Poring through his library of leather-bound volumes, the Greek could immerse himself in history so ancient that Roman times were considered recent. In his beloved land, from Mt. Olympus in the north, the fabled home of Zeus, Athena, Apollo and Aphrodite, the ancients had spread their Golden Age. Here the Olympic Games began, the slim, lithe athletes competing for the sheer glory of perfection. Here Plato and

Aristotle thought, and Socrates drained his cup of bitter hemlock to the lees. Here Thucydides and Herodotus wrote their histories, and Demosthenes overcame his speech impediment with a mouthful of stones to become one of the greatest orators of all time. Here Praxiteles sculpted the translucent Parian marble into shapes more heroically divine than human. Here Alexander the Great seized the reigns of power from Philip, his dying father, and marched across the civilized world to his immortal place in history. Here a tiny band of Spartans fought and fell at Thermopylae, linking forever the words "courage" and "Spartan." Onassis read on.

Here Homer wrote the Iliad, chronicalling the courage of Queen Penelope, weaving Laertes' shroud by day and unwinding it by night to delay her voracious suitors as she waited years for her wandering husband, Ulysses. Well versed in the *Iliad*, Onassis frequently quoted *Ulysses* to his friends. He must have enjoyed visiting Ithaca, where Ulysses finally returned home to draw the bow only he was capable of bending, to speed an arrow through twelve axe handles, and to systematically destroy his greedy rivals, fighting side by side with his faithful son, Telemachus.

The poet Tennyson once wrote of Ulysses, "Come, my friends, 'tis not too late to seek a newer world . . . to sail beyond the sunset and the baths of all the western stars until I die." The Greek shipmaster identified with the wanderlust of the Greek sea world, and with his dream of the *Christina* realized, and never ever having to depend upon the vicissitudes of commercial ships ever again, Onassis now could visit his beloved Greek Isles, drinking in the history he so deeply loved at *his* own leisure, staying and moving on when it suited *his* purposes.

This vital and lusty man, Zorba-like, the very personification of all tings Greek, sailed from one island to another—here Khalki, site of Aristotle's death; there pine-scented Samos, home of the ancient mathematician, Pythagoras, charting the roundness of the Earth, and where, centuries later, in history overlaid on history, the English poet, Lord Byron, would lose his life fighting for Greek independence.

Onassis might have walked the island of Lesbos, once the home of Sappho, the great lyric poetess, or strolled through the fabled tangerine groves of Vathis, perhaps plucking a handful of the zippered-skin fruit for his enjoyment. On Kos, Onassis could have stood beneath the wide arms of a plane tree, envisioning Hippocrates as he taught his first classes in medicine, draped in the white robes of the ancient Greeks. A few miles away, Onassis may have visited the Temple of Askelpios, an ancient three-tiered hospital where bodies were not only healed, but systematic research was conducted.

Climbing back aboard the sleek-prowed *Christina*, Onassis may have sailed for Ikaria, and stared at the sky, remembering that here the fabled Icarus attempted his flight to the sun, only to hurtle to the earth as the sun melted the wax of his feeble wings. Or, he may have sailed to Delos and treaded softly on earth so sacred to the ancients that laws were passed to prevent births and deaths from taking place on the island. He could have poked around the rocky hills, filled with ruins of columned palaces, theatres and temples, their Corinthian columns staring up brokenly from the debris. Incredible mosaics remain in the rubble, and Onassis may have stared in wonder at beautiful depictions of graceful dolphins leaping through the deep waters of the Aegean with small boys on their backs like Greek cowboys. Perhaps Onassis drew from these mosaics other ideas for fantastic floors and walls on his dream yacht.

Sailing on to the island of Sifnos, Onassis may have examined the ruins of the ancient gold mines which once poured out treasures for the entire ancient sea world. The Oracle at Delphi, it is said, once demanded in tribute a nugget of gold the size of an ostrich egg, but the greedy island sent instead a gold-painted rock. Angry at the treachery, the Oracle predicted a tragic end to the mines. In time, true to prediction, the sea flooded the shafts, wiping out the island's source of great wealth.

After a short voyage to Mikanos, Onassis could have enjoyed the round, soft-domed thatched windmills and those box-like houses, white-washed and gleaming in Aegean sun so bright it seems to light up the whole world. Perhaps the shipmaster stopped with friends at the local taverna for a sumptuous dinner of *barbounia,* the juicy red mullet of the Aegean, washing it down with ouzo, the milky, licorice-flavored drink of the islands. He might have roamed about some of the four hundred shrines and churches of this tiny island, built mostly for the protection of the sailors against the vagaries of the often-violent sea. Onassis, the sailor, would have understood that.

Reveling in his passion for history, Onassis would have seen the contrast between the white Greek Orthodox churches and the broken statues of gods and goddesses. For, as soon as the Apostle Paul journeyed across the straits and up Mars Hill, speaking with fiery eloquence about the Greeks' "Unknown God," whom Paul described as the One God "in whom we live and move and have our being," Greek history began to change. The old gods began to fade away with the new Christian churches in Thessalonica, Ephesus, Philippi, and the sin-sick city of Corinth. Suddenly islands so sacred to Zeus and Apollo were transformed into Christian sanctuaries. With one stroke, the Roman Emperor Domitian banished St. John to the Island of Patmos, turning it into a spot sacred to all Christians. Onassis may have visited the cave where the "beloved disciple" heard a great voice, "as of a trumpet," instructing him "what thou seest, write in a book, and send it unto the seven churches." As John obeyed, the Revelation of John was penned. Onassis may have stood in this rocky cavern, now filled with wondrous treasures, paintings encased in gold, crosses and silk embroideries, and, holiest of all, a silver arc encircling a smooth concave rock where St. John is believed to have lain his head. Perhaps he recalled the Christian legend that John, carried about on the shoulders of early Christians in his infirm years, would tenderly speak to everyone he met in a voice as sweet as love itself, over and over again, "Love one another; love one another; love one another."

Climbing upwards above the cave, Onassis could have visited the monastery of St. John, repository of some of the most precious Christian art in the world. Here rest vestments studded with pearls, gold crowns, gem-encrusted crosses and chalices, Bibles with covers of solid gold, all behind doors locked with three different locks, keys carried by three separate monks. Here, too, lies the Codex Purpureus, a portion of the Gospel of St. Mark, painstakingly inscribed in silver ink on purple vellum. Perhaps Onassis looked with loving eyes at these precious icons and parchments. But even with all his wealth, he would not have been able to purchase any one of them to add to his collection for his bedroom wall.

And so, he would have moved on to the Island of Rhodes, once the home of the Christian crusaders, indicative of yet another era of Greek history. Here, on moat walls once running red with the blood of Crusaders and their Islamic antagonists, Onassis would have enjoyed brilliant flowerfalls of scarlet bougainvillea.

As Aristotle Onassis plied his yacht about his islands, he would have certainly been struck, over and over again, with pride for this ancient land, a mosaic of history, of religions ancient and modern, of advanced learning, of incredibly beautiful art and music, of democracy, of his peoples' spirit, undaunted by invaders, whether they be human or the crashing waves of the sea. Onassis may have noted with pride the little island of Paxos, where, it is rumored, a Greek submarine hid in a secret cave, sallying forth on raids under the very noses of the Nazis. Perhaps he even smiled to himself at his countrymen's joke, no doubt humming a chorus of the Hymn to Liberty, the *Elevtherian,* under his breath.

And, no matter how far Onassis sailed on his quest for gold and power, he was always drawn, inexorably, back to Greece and his heritage. His bloodlines made it imperative; his *Christina* made it pleasant.

7

Wheels

Mrs. Twombly's Violet Rolls-Royce

In those halcyon days before the internal combustion engine, the gentle rich traveled in carriages drawn by the most beautiful horses their money would purchase. Often the horses were housed with the same elegance as their owners. Oliver Hazard Perry Belmont, for example, loved his equine friends so much that they were stabled on the first floor of the house in which he, himself, lived. Fragrant straw was changed many times a day, and, at night, sheets of Irish linen with the Belmont crest embroidered in the corners were laid over the straw, apparently in case the animals might want to lie down to rest. In Alfred Vanderbilt's stables, solid gold plates engraved with the horse's name were fastened to each stall door. And many consummately wealthy folks at the turn of the century, like Jay Gould, owned so many carriages that many of them might pass a whole year without being used once.

The rowdy and flamboyant Jim Fisk had his

own notions of elegance. Like a master painter, he assembled his rig. When most others drove a paltry four-in-hand, Jim selected six black and white horses, all perfectly matched, and supplied them with gold plated harnesses. The carriage, elegant by even those days' standards, was upholstered with gold silk cloth. And, to complete this perfect portrait, Jim ordered two black grooms dressed in white livery to ride the two lead horses, while two white footmen dressed in black ate dust at the rear. Fisk's arrival at the opera or some fancy party was always accomplished with the flair of a set of ebony and ivory dominoes.

Soon, however, the noisy automobiles began chugging and coughing into the lives of the rich. A few adventurous souls espoused the Tin Lizzie right away, while others, more conservative, refused them admission to their sacred grounds by reason that it disturbed the peace. Down in Palm Beach, automobiles were strictly *verboten,* and to get around, a strange vehicle was invented called an afromobile. This altogether luxurious conveyance was built rather like a three-wheeled Americanized rickshaw. Its seats of curlicued wicker were plushly cushioned, and the ladies and their small fry would ride about in comfort, daintily holding a parasol to ward off the damaging rays of the sun, while they were pushed wherever they chose to go by a long-suffering servant.

Chugging down the narrow rails of the 19th century, opening up a nation and stuffing wealth into the pockets of the railroad barons, railroad cars jostled and bumped the average citizen. But back in the private cars, insulated from overcrowding and noise, the super-rich traveled in an opulence carefully tailored for each whim and desire.

One winter day in the train yards, there was more activity and excitement than usual. Five different private cars must be readied and hooked up before the Gould party arrived. Working in the snow and cold, care must be taken by the workmen not to allow any smudges on the white velvet or the polished brass. Eventually all was ready and the workmen waited with expectancy.

Finally they arrived, the whole Gould family and their guests. Fur capes and velvet muffs of the ladies swept past into the cars, already heated to a toasty warmth. The winter sports carnival in Quebec was waiting, and they would have as much fun getting there as they would watching the Canadian skaters.

Chefs, butlers, valets and ladies' maids were already in attendance. The chefs had begun to prepare the gourmet meals of caviar, canvasback duck, and Maryland terrapin, the de rigeur menus in those days. Back in the enormous pantry lay the fixings for future meals of foie gras, pheasant, broiled squab, quail, and broiled oysters. And, although Jay Gould did not personally drink, he had made certain the wine cellar was filled with the finest stock. Up in the china closet, the Gould's own private gold table service was polished and waiting.

Back in the sumptuous sleeping cars, the maids had replaced the common sheets with the

Gould's own silken linen, and they had laid away the evening clothes brought especially for the elegant dinners aboard the train.

In the parlor car, family and guests sat giggling and chatting as the train pulled away from the station. They were surrounded by the heaviest cut velvet with drooping tassels, all in gleaming white, matching the snowy landscape of upstate New York in midwinter.

At intervals on the trip, Jay Gould and his men friends could adjourn to the club car, away from the delicate noses of the ladies, to smoke hefty Havanas and to trim up mustaches and burnsides in the barber's chair installed under an arching dome of stained glass. Later they might join the ladies in the observation car, all glass, viewing the winter sunsets and snowbanks in perfect, warm luxury.

Before dressing in those white ties and tails for dinner, the guests could bathe in the train's own bathtub under a soaring ceiling decorated with Gothic fretwork. After leisurely dressing, each would join the other elegants in their silks and satins for a crystal goblet of champagne. It somehow makes the destination seem a trifle unimportant.

By the 1920's, these private railroad cars were going for $300,000 each. This is equal to today's private jets, at least in price, if not in luxury. Individual whims and desires were perfectly expressed in these cars made to order. Going the Gould's vermeil table service one better, one lady decided to install solid gold plumbing fixtures. She decided it was a definite economy, as it saved "all that terrible polishing."

Lily Langtry's private car, a gift from a very wealthy admirer of the theatre arts, held a mammoth food locker. The famous actress described it as being so huge that it would "hold a whole stag." Others held extensive wine bins, and most held hidden jewel safes to protect the diamonds and gems of the ladies. Ornate Victorian organs were often installed, in those days before juke boxes and Muzak, to accord the families a musical concert.

Often families attached other private cars to fulfill their various needs. Louis Hill always had one other car to be used only as a garage holding his automobile, replete with bedrooms for his chauffeur and mechanic. The Gould's special cow, again tested for just the right butterfat, traveled in her own car, supplying fresh milk and cream for the morning strawberries. Somehow this seems even more luxurious than James Gordon Bennett's seagoing cow. After all, one *can* get off a train to milk a cow.

Cissy Patterson, publisher of the Washington Times-Herald, was an advocate of variety in her life. She had seven different sets of slipcovers prepared for every piece of furniture in her private car, one for every day of the week, and all seven would be brought to the train before her arrival. Then, each morning, while Cissy slept, her butler would see to it that a different set was installed. Cissy awoke to a new world every day of her life.

Mrs. Patterson was also inordinately fond of flowers and insisted that she be surrounded by their luxurious beauty day and night. Florists

along the railroad right of way were tele-
graphed, advising them of her needs. As she
pulled into each station, there they sat, whole
wagons full of blossoms, ready to fulfill her
desires of having fresh blooms cover every
conceivable surface in her private car.

As soon as Mr. Rolls and Mr. Royce began
building their fine limousines at Crewe,
England, they ushered in an age of elegance and
luxury in motoring theretofore unknown. No
other automobile even approaches the status of
owning one of these incredible cars. Handmade
to amazingly close tolerances and painted with
many rubbed coats, the very name *Rolls-Royce*
epitomizes the ultimate in quality.

Church bells rang out a pealing summons of
Sunday morning. As good folk ascended the
stairs to enter the sanctuary, a legendary sight
greeted their eyes.

Down the street purred a silver and violet
Rolls-Royce, polished to perfection, its
chauffeur neatly uniformed in natty black coat,
tie, hat, with white gloves, carefully steering the
leather wheel. He drew to the curb and jumped
out, adjusting his hat as he went. Opening the
rear door, he stood at attention, offering his
hand to the occupant.

Suddenly, she stepped out, Mrs. Hamilton
Twombly, the granddaughter of old Commodore
Cornelius Vanderbilt, elegant as always, dressed
in a matching violet dress, and carrying a
bouquet of hothouse violets.

Without a backward glance, Mrs. Twombly

strode up the steps to worship in her private pew, knowing, but never indicating that she knew, the satisfactory effect her coordinated costume and automobile had on the astonished onlookers.

As with yachts and private railroad cars, the Rolls-Royce is always customized to the tastes of its fantastically wealthy owner. Mrs. Twombly, herself, had a gold and emerald-encrusted vanity installed to use in powdering her nose, which, cost her at the time, $10,000. Mink lap robes were a favorite accessory. Personalized Rolls-Royces often contained jeweled clocks in the dashboards, and bars of rare woods, with carefully controlled refrigeration for wines, held crystal tumblers by Baccarat for drinking them. Gentlemen whose passions included fine cigars had the option to install air conditioned humidors to protect the freshness of their stogies. One gentleman even had the ceiling of his fine Silver Shadow painted like some contemporary Sistine Chapel on wheels! Another gentle lady had her Rolls upholstered with a priceless Aubusson needlework tapestry. The fabric alone cost her $3,000 in late 1920's currency. Sometimes crystal vases were attached to the walls near the hang strap, and held one perfect, creamy-pink American Beauty rose, which was scrupulously replaced by the chauffeur at the slightest indication of wilting.

Chauffeurs received their instructions over a private telephone line between wheel and passenger's seat. It would be, after all, considered quite gauche to yell back and forth.

A very strict ritualized set of do's and don't's have been set forth for these Rolls-Royce chauffeurs. Unequivocally these men are excellent drivers; that goes without saying. But they also present a sense of dignity approaching that of the Great Stone Face. One would not even *consider* driving out of uniform, and absolutely *never* anything as oafish as resting one's elbow on the window ledge. It was the chauffeur's responsibility to see that the automobile was in perfect order, both mechanically and esthetically, at all times. To be certain not a speck of dust clouded the beauty, he often could be found during non-rolling times, polishing the bonnet and flying hood ornament with a dustrag of perfectly matched mink skins!

8

A Generous Heart

J. P. Morgan Saves a Bank

The big miner with the drooping Yosemite Sam mustache shuffled and looked down at the floor, oddly embarrassed. Only a few years out of a prospector's rough Levis, his finely tailored suit hung a trifle ill at ease on his tall frame. The young woman smiled at his discomfiture, tenderly, understanding.

The word of her loss and desperate financial need had circulated rapidly throughout Virginia City in the past few days, and John Mackay had been instantly concerned. The big man, twofifths owner of the fabulous Comstock Mine, was never one to allow widows and orphans to starve. He thrust a bank bag onto her kitchen table. It clanked heavily.

Western legend has it that she stared first at him and then at the bag, cheeks reddening and her eyes glistening with tears, her voice choking with emotion as she tried to express her thanks to this unlikely looking angel.

He waved off her thanks and turned to stump

toward the rough door, again embarrassed by the hooplah. But she wouldn't let him go, her pride needing to express her appreciation.

The young woman touched his arm and gestured toward the stove, where a meager meal simmered, and invited him to share their meal. He turned and stared at the half-empty pots for a moment before turning back to the widow, smiling and pulling out a chair to sit down. Moments later, the food was served, and the unlikely couple set to, as the widow shared of her own bounty with her benefactor.

Before the last bean was served, the stiffness between the two had begun to dissolve into a comfortable friendship, and before too many months had passed, John Mackay was back with hat in hand. Formally, in the style of the old West, he asked for her hand in marriage. The scene must have been very tender, this rough miner and his hoped-for bride. Both had shared what each had; he had a golden wealth, and she only a meager supper, but both gifts were now to be blessed and multiplied, in loving union.

"I'll always take care of you," John Mackay is said to have vowed, "even if I have to dig a living with my bare hands."

For the rest of his life, John was to live up to that promise, and he cared for his new wife and her family, protectively, royally. Together they traveled the silk-tasseled, gilt private railroad cars to the East, boarding a luxury liner for Europe, and hobnobbed with royalty who were delighted at the simple freshness of these two good people. Mrs. Mackay dined at the best restaurants in satins and lace, never to be hungry again.

Yet they always remembered to share. Mackay continued to give of his abundant overflow, millions upon millions of dollars to others less fortunate, always given under the strictest vow of secrecy. And, as he continued to give, he continued to be blessed. Fortunes in the mining business might change quickly for some, but for John Mackay, the windows of heaven were always open and he amassed a fortune undreamt of even in the legendary grandeur of the American West.

The miner realized very early in life that, along with the luxuries—jaunts across Europe with kings and princes, eccentric spending sprees, and legendary homes—which vast wealth can supply, money also carries with it obligation. Money equals power, and, as with everything else, it can be used for good or ill.

Insurance mogul Clement Stone has decried his inability to doctor to the blind and lepers, or to minister to those in foreign countries, but he realized that his money can go where he physically cannot. Sending his vast bounty forth, hospitals were built, leprosariums were raised, men healed and comforted. For as Stone has aptly stated, without money, there wouldn't be any hospitals and the blind would not see.

If money has the power to heal, it also has the ability to sway governments, and sometimes in *positive* ways! At the turn of the century, news flashed across the world on telegraphs and rusty-sounding telephones. The battleship *Maine* had exploded in Havana harbor. The

United States was at war.

Back home in New York, Mrs. Jay Gould was irate. American soliders were getting shot up in some smelly little harbor thousands of miles away. Men were dying. Bullets and food were in short supply. Penicillin and quinine to fight the infections of tropical battlefields were nonexistent. Something *must* be done!

The next day, the beautiful library at Lyndhurst was crowded with ladies. No china teacups this day, no flaky French pastries, no chamber music. Sixty ladies of position sat, some sewing, their needles flashing in and out, others ripping rags into bandages, knitting mufflers, their elegant morning dresses covered with lint and threads.

Meanwhile, Mrs. Gould fumed long distance at a U.S. Senator over the old-fashioned black telephone. These things *will be* on the next boat, she vowed. So why isn't the government getting supplies down there? The boys *need* things, she harrumphed, and there's no reason for the government to hem and haw around, letting them suffer.

The Senator murmured a polite response, but Mrs. Gould was not through. The ladies' sewing needles stopped abruptly at the next bit of news. "There's a $100,000 bank draft on the way to your office, made payable to the United States government. Use it any way you can to get this war over and our boys home!"

The Senator's gulp was probably clearly audible in his office, although not in Mrs. Gould's ear over the turn-of-the-century telephone, but his answer was. "Yes, Ma'am!"

In a couple of weeks, when wounded soldiers began pouring back into New York harbor, Mrs. Gould was again on the scene. No place for them? The very idea! Not if *she* could help it. Yanking on an elegant velvet bellrope to summon her butler, she vowed to *make* a place. The door opened and Mrs. Gould was issuing orders before the hapless butler got halfway into the room. So many things to be done—store the furniture in the New York house, order new beds, send someone for doctors and medicine. If the government couldn't do it, then *she* would. Within days, one of her expensive New York homes was transformed into a hospital for the "boys."

Mrs. Gould fussed at the government all during the Spanish-American War, muttering that she believed she could win this war better and faster herself. Telephone lines hummed between New York and Washington as the dauntless lady cajoled and threatened, argued and persuaded. Not until the last bullet was fired and the last American soldier safely home did this woman of indomitable courage and energy and bottomless wealth cease her work.

Some governmental obligations of the very rich have nothing to do with gifts of money. Sometimes other sacrifices are required.

In 1937, Hitler's armies were poised at the brink of Austria, hovering like some great, leering jackal, waiting to spread the poison of anti-Semitism and swallow up Europe in one gulp. Jews, both poor and high-born, waited with leaden dread and uncertainty. What would

111

be their fate? Most certainly every one of them was in the direst danger. Many with sufficient wealth to travel had already fled to the comparative safety of Switzerland or Paris.

Back at the Renngasse in Vienna, in an elegant office richly canopied in dark red silk, the Baron Louis Rothschild looked up from the hand-carved desk as a yellow-and-blue-armbanded courier from the Paris House of Rothschild came in.

The Baron must leave; it was too dreadfully dangerous for him to stay, surely Herr Baron must see that. Every day's delay thrust them closer to disaster. As a Jew, and as the epitome of Jewish capitalism, Rothschild represented all that Der Fuehrer despised most. The Baron would certainly be one of the first to die.

Typically, Louis Rothschild's back must have stiffened, his patrician eyebrow raised, his silver head tilted back in a gesture of aristocratic defiance. *This* was a matter of *principle*. This House of Rothschild had *always* been allied with the government of Austria. During the depression years, much of the Rothschild fortune had been liquidated and contributed to bolster the government and keep it from toppling. Time and again, Rothschild influence and wealth had stabilized Vienna, so tenuously holding her grip on a faltering country. For the Baron to leave now, with the German invasion imminent, would mean certain collapse of the government.

No, this was a matter of principle; Herr Baron would *not* leave. The courier bowed, his forehead furrowed with worry, and scurried out, anxious to be away, back to Paris and safety.

Following on the courier's heels, the Baron strode casually to his limousine and, moments later, was on his way, perhaps to a museum to enjoy precious paintings in full view of fellow Austrians, or maybe to the stables of the alabaster Lippizaners for a mid-afternoon session of dressage. With the horse poised in an agonizingly difficult, perfect levade, the Baron Rothschild was in complete control of his animal and of himself.

For weeks, Herr Baron fearlessly, aristocratically moved about Vienna, keeping a very high profile with all the elan of a D'Artagnon, flashing steel in the teeth of evil.

In March of 1938, German troops goose-stepped across the border. Despite Baron Louis Rothschild's valiant attempt to throw all the strength and prestige of his illustrious house behind the government of Austria, all was lost. Finally, with all hope gone, this great man at last allowed himself to be driven to the airport.

The scene was one of panic; long lines crushing against ticket windows; people begging to be allowed aboard a plane, any plane, no matter where. The Baron strode through the crowd, characteristically untouched by the turmoil. At the last moment, a sneering S.S. officer tapped him on the shoulder, holding out his hand for the Rothschild passport. With an icy stare and a curt bow, the Baron handed it over and turned away. All that was left to do now was to wait.

That night, two men flashing the hated swastika on their sleeves pounded on the door, their boots gleaming in the soft light streaming from the Baron's windows. With all the aplomb of years of service to aristocracy, the butler opened the door.

Herr Baron, if you please. The ruffians grinned evilly and tapped their obscene armbands. In an incredible display of courage, the butler announced that he must see if the Herr Baron was in, leaving the two astonished men to cool their heels in the marbled hall. Returning some minutes later, he bowed politely and announced solemnly, so sorry, the Baron is *not* at home.

The insolent grins faded into shock and disbelief, and the two stuttering Nazis fled into the dark. But the next day, Sunday, March 13, 1938, they were back, with reinforcements, guns drawn, faces grim.

"We will let him go upon payment of $200,000, sir. And, of course, all of the assets of the Austrian House of Rothschild." Herman Goering's advisor smiled thinly as he delivered this demand deep in the bowels of the Gestapo headquarters. He inhaled deeply on a harsh cigarette. His hands itched for the treasures that would belong to the Third Reich. Vitkovitz! The largest iron and coal works in Central Europe! It would be invaluable to the war effort, fueling the awesome Panzer Divisions rolling across a crushed Europe. And it would be all theirs in exchange for this worthless Jew.

But the Baron's lips must have parted in that incredibly cool, arrogant smile. For, in those tense days while Germany hulked on the border,

Rothschild had transferred ownership of Vitkovitz to England. It was beyond the dark grasp of the Reich! He would win after all. D'Artagnon lived!

Sometimes these enormous gambles pay off. J. P. Morgan's nose, as round and red as W. C. Field's, commanded his face only degrees ahead of his piercing blue eyes. Cold the eyes may have seemed at first glance, but they were reported to have hidden a heart of kindness and generosity.

Morgan scanned the sheets on his desk and frowned, shaking his head and muttering about the risk. Representatives of the two failing banks must have dropped their shoulders and stared down at their hands in despondency.

"Who are the main depositors here?" he reportedly asked as he glanced over the top of the balance sheets at the two men.

Poor people, mostly, was the answer; East-siders, about 30,000 of them. If these two banks were to fail, it would mean the end of everything these working class folks had struggled for.

According to Morgan legend, there was deep silence in the cigar-smelling offices of the bank. On one side of the room, Morgan's vice presidents waited, confident that he wouldn't jeopardize millions in such a foolhardy manner. On the far side of the room, the other two men held their breath, hoping against all possible hope that, by some miracle, Morgan would see a glimmer of merit in their request.

"Some way must be found to help those poor people," the financier finally murmured. "We mustn't let them lose all they have in the world." Morgan glanced back at the balance sheet, apparently making some rapid calculations in his head. How much were they talking about? What was the most he could lose?

Six million dollars.

Six million dollars? "You mean to tell me that's *all* I can lose?" Morgan is supposed to have answered. Done. The guaranty forms were laid on his desk and Morgan whipped out a great black fountain pen to sign them with a flourish.

The prestige of an important banker worked; the banks were saved, and Morgan's six million dollar loss was unnecessary after all.

One of the more flamboyant rescues of a bank concerns Ned Green, the millionaire son of old Hetty Green, the legendary "Witch of Wall Street."

One sun-drenched day in Dallas, Ned was having breakfast with his good friend, Edward Harper, president of the Dallas Security National Bank. Fresh flowers graced the table, and icy droplets rolled down the sides of the crystal water glasses. Green and Harper were in fine settle, sipping sweet glasses of orange juice squeezed moments earlier by hand.

Suddenly, shattering the conviviality of the moment, a messenger arrived. Hurry, he urged, his shaking hands tugging at Harper's sleeve. There was a run on the bank, more money was needed; they'd all be ruined!

As the bank president rose, white-faced, to grapple with the problem, Ned merely waved him back to his seat. It was not necessary for his friend to become alarmed, or even to interrupt

116

his breakfast. How much was needed? Green reached into his breast pocket and pulled forth a wallet stuffed with a wad of bills. He counted out twenty $10,000 bills and shoved them across the table.

Not enough? No problem. Green beckoned to the bellboy and sent him scurrying to Ned's hotel room for a battered old suitcase perching casually on the bed.

When Ned opened it at the table in full view of the entire restaurant, the bank president nearly choked. It was crammed full of $10,000 bills, spilling out over the sides! Ned pulled out another thirty bills and handed them to his friend, not bothering to ask for a receipt, then motioned to the waiter to bring on the sausages.

One of the greatest philanthropists in recent history was John D. Rockefeller, Jr. He had learned from his father that money was a gift from God and man only the trustee, with the responsibility to distribute the money in wise ways, as investments in the "well-being of mankind." Rockefeller's vast resources went to Save the Redwoods in California at time before ecology became a national consciousness.

After World War I, he was distressed by the bomb-ravaged ruins of the beautiful palace at Versailles. Roaming about the Petit Trianon where Marie Antoinette gamboled before her bloody demise, Rockefeller could have sensed the history of this lovely place which had touched an entire world. Here the Treaty of Paris was signed, ending the American Revolutionary War. Here William was proclaimed Emperor of Germany, the heavy, ornate Prussian uniforms gleaming in the kaleidoscope of the Hall of Mirrors. Here, among the rubble, the peace ending World War I was drawn, to the collective sighs of an entire earth. Rockefeller opened his cash box again and out came the funds to rebuild this architectural and cultural treasure of France.

But for all the dollars given to conservation, museums and education, the one project closest to John D. Rockefeller, Jr.'s heart and the one which has captured a grateful nation's imagination has been the restoration of Williamsburg.

In 1923, a visionary man named Rev. William Goodwin returned to Williamsburg to accept a post as a professor and as Director of the Endowment Plan of the College of William and Mary. Twenty years earlier, Dr. Goodwin had been rector of the Bruton Parish Church, and had spent five years restoring this beautiful old house of worship which had been brutalized by the ravages of time and the vacillating fancies of generations of parishioners.

This good man returned to his beloved Williamsburg and stared in disbelief at the deterioration caused by modern life. Telephone lines snaked across the sky in ugly webs, gasoline pumps glowed in the dark, billboards and advertising splashed their garishness across the streets and along the sides of shabby buildings. Time was running out for Williamsburg.

But Dr. Goodwin walked the streets at night when no one else was around. He marched with the ghosts of American ancestors who had written freedom, fought for freedom, died for freedom. Here Patrick Henry thundered, and Thomas Jefferson scrawled with quill pen his Statute for Religious Freedom. It was a heritage which *mustn't* be allowed to crumble into dust.

With the help of the Association for the Preservation of Virginia Antiquities, Dr. Goodwin found money to restore several old buildings. But he realized this was a project too vast in scope for a piecemeal plan and his limited resources, and he began looking around for a benefactor.

In 1924, Dr. Goodwin spoke at a Phi Beta Kappa banquet in New York, and he noticed the great financier, John D. Rockefeller, Jr., sitting some ways down the table. The man's eyes seemed to take on a far-away look as he raptly listened to Dr. Goodwin's personal adventures in the musty archives and history-soaked buildings.

Two years later, in 1926, Dr. Goodwin was ushered into the office of the president of the College of William and Mary. The excited look on the executive's face indicated something special was up. Great news! John D. Rockefeller, Jr., was coming to Williamsburg! Would Dr. Goodwin consent to be his guide?

Would he! What a wonderful opportunity! Dr. Goodwin made each street come alive. With his inspired, enthusiastic words, the garish street signs faded, the telephone lines disappeared, modern dress dissolved into farthingales and knee breeches. The two men began to see Williamsburg as it had been two centuries before, and could be again.

The scent of woodsmoke wafted through their nostrils, some Colonial dame was cooking Smithfield ham and peanut soup. The sounds of fife and drum—the militia marched up and down the Green. Heels clicked on the Duke of Glouchester Street; if they'd looked behind, perhaps they would have seen Patrick Henry hurrying to the Hall of the House of Burgesses to deliver his famous Caesar-Brutus speech, his voice thundering out the silver tones of freedom. A softer sound this time, metal against wood, and a craftsman was carving a delicate shell motif into the front of some mahogany desk, the curls of wood peeling off and floating to the ground. From the inn, the sound of a lute rang out, with the voice of the minstrel singing a love ballad in a sad minor key.

From further away, a spinning wheel's rhythmic creak was accented by the periodic whump of a loom, as indigo-dyed wool cloth inched off in patterns older than America. Here and there a whiff of lavender floated downwind on a breeze from the gardener's workshop where herbs were being tied together and hung upside down in rafters to dry. A woman's low laugh was overshadowed by the high pealing giggles of children running by in long skirts and breeches, the pewter buckles on their brogues glittered dully, their hands crammed with soft, chewy gingerbread freshly out of the brick ovens. And, down the street from the forge came a sudden hiss as the smith plunged a red-glowing wagon tire into a waiting bucket of water.

At the Wythe House, Dr. Goodwin introduced

Rockefeller to George Parsons, the black caretaker. George smiled and dropped a handful of square, handmade nails into Rockefeller's palm, a 200-year-old memento. He stared at them for some time before silently turning away. What thoughts were racing through Rockefeller's mind? Dr. Goodwin scarcely dared to hope.

Later, Rockefeller asked if he might roam the grounds alone, to think. Swallowing his excitement, Dr. Goodwin graciously withdrew and silently watched as the philanthropist slowly moved down the street, staring at the buildings, pausing to stare up at a giant, gnarled mulberry tree, running his hands over its bizarre beauty, lost in a world only he could see.

Shortly thereafter, Rockefeller authorized preliminary work on the project. For over a year, he and Dr. Goodwin worked in strictest secrecy, no one knowing the name of this mysterious benefactor. The plan was so vast, the possibilities for failure so infinite, that Rockefeller desired his name not be used until it was assured that the total plan could be achieved.

Houses were bought, maps compared, preliminary sketches prepared, obstacles overcome. And still Rockefeller's name was never mentioned.

Finally, in June of 1928, the citizens of Williamsburg met in a great town meeting and, with a dramatic pause, Dr. Goodwin announced, "It is now my very great privilege and pleasure to announce that the donors of the money to restore Williamsburg are Mr. and Mrs. John D. Rockefeller, Jr., of New York."

After the cheering died down, work began in

earnest. The project grew in size and scope and, with each completed building, several new ones were discovered to be restored. Rockefeller spent as much time as possible in the little village, watching his dream unfold. Through it all, he insisted on absolute honesty in every detail. Everything must be authentic, down to the last nail, the last fife, the last deck of cards.

One day, workmen discovered that a house which they had already started to reconstruct was about six feet off its original position. To move it now would cost another $6,000. What to do? After all, it was *only* six feet off.

After some discussion it was decided to ask Mr. Rockefeller, who was again visiting the work site. His brows must have furrowed in a slight frown. "Why, gentlemen," he is reported as saying, "why are you asking *me* about *this*? Of course the house should be moved."

This absolute adherence to perfection characterized the work from beginning to end, and now Americans can trudge through the streets and feel their roots, their link with a country dedicated from its inception to the rights of humanity, freedom, and equality. During World War II, American soldiers were often given trips through Williamsburg, and many times it produced a heightened sense of loyalty and realization of what principles he would be fighting for once he stepped onto the soil of Europe.

Today, millions of Americans silently bless Rockefeller's foresight and generosity as they walk through the streets of their history, touching the faded old bricks of the Bruton

Parish Church, or running their fingers over the highly polished cherrywood of an elegant sideboard fashioned by some long-dead forebear, listening to the plaintive lute and harpsichord, or strolling through the sweetly-scented formal gardens of the Elkanah Deane House and the Governor's Mansion.

The art of giving has been developed to a fine art by many wealthy men. The Astor's are responsible for building a home for emotionally disturbed children and a playground for poor children in the Bronx; J. P. Morgan managed to consistently invent jobs for the elderly or the ill so they could retain some pride at having earned their own way; the Rothschild's have sustained French ballet and Israeli craftsmen and have given generously to education for American Indians; John Mackay's most famous gifts are the Mackay School of Mines in Reno, Nevada, and the Church of St. Mary's of the Mountain in Virginia City, Colorado; Andrew Mellon gave the East Building of the National Gallery of Art in Washington, D.C., as a gift to the people of the United States.

The DuPont's turned their fabulous home, Nemours, into a center for the cure of crippled children. Pierre DuPont is renown for millions of dollars given for education. M.I.T., the University of Delaware, the University of Virginia, and the University of Pennsylvania have all drunk thirstily of DuPont generosity. And Lincoln University, a black school in Pennsylvania, has also received endowments from the DuPont trust.

The family has, in addition, turned most of its other historic homes and gardens into museums. For example, the one thousand acres of Longwood Gardens is run by a thirty-three million dollar trust to ensure that the public will always be allowed to enjoy these formal gardens which blooms all the growing season of the year.

On a more personal level, Aristotle Onasis was fond of giving in great measure to his good friends. Nothing was too difficult or expensive if it pleased a friend of the Greek shipmaster.

Late in Winston Churchill's life, he became close friends with Onassis. What an odd couple the two made; Churchill, the brilliant statesman and Nobel Prize winner, beloved by the western world, and Onassis, the ebullient Greek of sometimes dubious reputation. Despite the world's criticism, the two developed a friendship which lasted until Sir Winston's death. The father-son relationship was said to have been a tender and gentle thing to behold, Onassis rushing to wait hand and foot on the old gentleman, bringing him a blanket to ward off the sea's chill, or another glass of Dom Perignon.

If the sea became too choppy for the old man's comfort, Onassis phoned the bridge with orders for the captain to meet him in Sir Winston's cabin on the double. There, together, they would adjust the speed of the opulent yacht until the ship's vibrations ceased or were at their precise minimum.

One day, while Onassis and Churchill were in the midst of one of their endless conversations on history or philosophy, the old man's palsied hand shook, dumping a caviar-laden cracker onto his lap. Without missing a syllable of debate, Onassis merely dragged his chair over to Sir Winston's and began feeding him mouthful after mouthful of the succulent caviar, gentle as a father with his child.

Onassis' tables were often laden with the riches of the sea and the luscious cuisine of Greece; lamb, savory with herbs and olive oil, stuffed grape leaves and *baklava*, that sweet, tender pastry which flakes off in a hundred pieces at the touch of a silver fork and melts in one's mouth.

One fine blue-gold day in the Aegean, a cook came to Onassis and Churchill, interrupting their endless debate to discuss the menu for the evening. Churchill happened to mention that, in all his trips to Greece, he had never once tasted *baklava*.

A slight smile must have passed over Onassis face; here was another special gift he could give his friend. Slipping away for a moment, he whispered to his pilot, who sped away to the seaplane, revving up and flying off to the middle of Greece to find the finest bakery. That night, after all the other succulent courses were served, the chef marched in with great ceremony, placing fresh *baklava* at Churchill's plate.

Churchill was no fool; he certainly realized the enormous lengths to which his friend had gone to supply him with this tiny desire. Something must be done to show his appreciation. Years had taken their toll on the old man's body, but, weak and feeble as he was, Churchill stayed in his cabin all day, painting one of his marvelous landscapes. His hands shook, but no matter, *this* was important. That afternoon, very late, he phoned Tina Onassis, asking her to come to his cabin.

Smiling at the gift, she called the ship's carpenter, who hurriedly built a new frame for the painting, and then the three of them sneaked up to the Game Room to hang the landscape, unbeknownst to Onassis.

They waited for him there, smiling conspiratorially, and, when Ari walked in, he sniffed the air, quizzically. Had one of the workmen been painting? He could smell fresh paint. No one said a word, but glanced at each other, grinning.

Finally, Ari spotted the landscape. His mouth dropped open in delight and, according to sources, tears began to fill his eyes. Knowing the old man's frailty, the gesture was made even more important. He rushed to the old Prime Minister's side and the men embraced; the whole moment was a culmination of the unique friendship between these two disparate men.

Perhaps none of the wealthy enjoyed giving more than Sir Leopold de Rothschild, for it was said that his hand automatically reached for a pocket the very moment he spied a tyke coming towards him. This man of zestful enthusiasm for living always seemed to find ways to return his bounty to the world. An avid racehorse breeder, it was said that the more races he won, the more money he lost. In joyful celebration of a champion, he often would keep the silver loving cup and give the prize money away, often enough for some fortunate hospital to finance an entire new wing!

In the farflung Rothschild family, with its incredible wealth, its sons could do whatever they chose; Leopold chose horses and hospitals. But they could work in the family bank, collect precious objets d'art, grow orchids, run governments, research rare insects, or do nothing at all. But the Rothschild's were not a family to raise idlers. And Edmond Rothschild was, in every sense, a true Rothschild. He may, indeed, have been the inspiration for Baron Louis Rothschild's adamant resistance of Nazi invasion.

Scion of this family whose roots stretched back to the degradations of a Jewish ghetto in eighteenth century Germany, Edmond Rothschild tasted his Jewish heritage with every breath. It was to become for him an all-consuming passion. Confronted on a fateful day in 1882 by the visionary soul of Rabbi Samuel Mohilever, the idea of a modern Jewish homeland grasped him, and, for the next fifty years, never let him go. Centuries of anti-Semitic oppression were drawing rapidly to a climax. Hitler's holocaust was mere decades away. In Russia, Hasidic Jews were undergoing intolerable suffering already. It was time for a second Exodus. Moses' words reverberated down through the millenium, "Thus saith the Lord God of Israel, let my people go!" Edmond Rothschild heard the commandment.

During the rest of his life, Rothschild was to

give *tens of millions* of dollars to Jewish colonies in Palestine. He began by financing one small settlement of only one hundred and one Russian Jews near Jaffa. Soon Rothschild money began to be pipelined to save the few struggling Jewish colonies already established in Palestine, fore-sightedly clustered around Galilea, Samaria and Judea. The land started to bloom. Irrigation ditches were dug, homes built, almond trees and mulberries planted, vineyards established. The desert's air was scented with the sweet smell of jasmine and mint once again. Zion had begun.

Five years after the initial visit with Rabbi Mohilever, Rothschild finally visited Zion. One can imagine his excitement and anticipation at walking through Palestine, visiting the legendary lands of his heritage.

He went at once to Jerusalem, the holiest city of Moslems, Christians and Jews. Here, accor-ding to tradition, Abraham carried out prepara-tions to sacrifice Isaac, only to be spared this grief at the last moment. Here King David converted an ancient Jebusite town into his capital, Zion. Here, too, the angry prophet Nathan confronted David, accusing him of the murder of Uriah the Hittite in order to make Bathsheba his own. Here the son of David and Bathsheba, Solomon, prayed for a "wise and understanding heart," and built the Temple of the One God, drawing on all the wealth and opulence of ancient Tyre, importing its most skilled carpenters and stonemasons. Nothing but the finest would do for this Temple. With it, Solomon would show his thanksgiving to a God who had given him, not only the wise and understanding heart, but what he had not asked, "riches and honor, so that no other king shall compare with you, all your days." Cypress and the fabled cedars which Isaiah called "the glory of Lebanon" were shipped in to build the firmest foundation; bolts of finest linen dyed with the famed royal purple of Tyre were sent to drape the inside of the temple.

Then the great Temple fell, destroyed by the Babylonians. The Jews were carried into captivity, from which they sang a sad Psalm, "On the willows there we hung up our lyres, for there our captors required of us songs . . . how can we sing the Lord's song in a foreign land?" Rothschild understood the anguish.

Much later, King Herod was to rebuild the Temple on the foundations of the first, but Edmond Rothschild would see none of its wonder. For, within a century of the death of the man called Jesus, Romans would destroy the Temple again, leaving only a fragment of the Western Wall to remind Jews of the past glories of David's and Solomon's kingdoms—the famed Wailing Wall. Rothschild reacted as his brethren, throwing himself against the stones worn smooth by centuries of hands, and mourning for his fallen Israel.

In the days that followed, Edmond Rothschild was to attempt, unsuccessfully, to purchase the Wailing Wall from the Arabs. In retrospect, it might have been better had he been able to buy with money what has since been purchased with blood.

Everywhere Rothschild turned on that fateful expedition in 1887, he was confronted with his ancestry. He walked the Holy Land, incongruous in his velvet bow tie among coarsely woven robes. At Hebron, he may have visited the spot where tradition says Abraham and Sarah are entombed. He may have followed in the steps of Moses as he led the children of Israel out of the Land of Goshen across the Yam Suph, the Reed Sea. Perhaps Rothschild climbed Jabal Musa, thought by many to be the sacred Mt. Sinai, from which Moses brought down the tablets bearing the precious Ten Commandments which began to turn the ancient race from a tribe of avengers to one governed by Law. Surely Rothschild trod the land of Midian, where, while shepherding Jethro's flocks, Moses encountered God speaking to him through the Burning Bush. At Rephidim near Mt. Sinai, the great Jewish millionare may have imitated Moses, vainly trying to hold up his arms as the Israelites fought the Amalekites and won as Aaron propped up weary arms for the duration of the battle.

At Kadesh-Barnea, the Israelites' encampment for much of the "Wandering," Rothschild may have envisioned Moses waiting in anticipation for his scouts to return from Canaan. From the Valley of Eshcol near Hebron, it is written that the spies returned with bunches of grapes so large they had to be carried back on a pole between them. This was truly the land of milk and honey. Surely Rothschild must have wondered if his people would ever cross back into this modern promised land.

But Moses and Aaron were never to enter the Promised Land. On Mt. Nebo, Moses stared over into the land he had worked so hard to reach, and died. Aaron, his brother, too died—on Jabal Harun, the Mt. of Aaron, near the rose-red city of Petra, leaving Joshua to lead the people across the Jordan River into Canaan. Possibly Rothschild stood on these spots, feeling the anguish which the patriarchs must have felt at what they considered their failures.

Traveling further, Rothschild would have continued to meet his past at every turn. Jacob's Well; Mt. Tabor, where the prophetess Deborah watched as Sisera the Canaanite was defeated on the plains below; Mt. Gilboa, where Gideon's tiny army streamed down into the valley to smite the Midianites, and where the wicked Jezebel was eaten by dogs as her just reward; Mt. Megiddo, Solomon's fortress where so many crucial and bloody battles were fought that it justly earned the connotation of Armageddon, the "final confrontation". Further north, Rothschild may have visited ancient Sarepta where Elijah restored a Phoenician boy to life, or Byblos, a city whose precious parchment lent its name to the most famous book in history. Perhaps he visited Qumran, where the Essenes, a Jewish sect of mystics called the "Children of Light," prayed and copied their priceless manuscripts, one day to be discovered and dubbed the "Dead Sea Scrolls."

Without a doubt, Rothschild climbed Masada. Here on this mountain fortress, a handful of Jews held off Roman attacks until, with all hope gone, they died by their own hands, depriving the legions of this most bitter victory.

With Rothschild's millions poured into

making Israel a reality, he would have felt great joy and gratification that here, on this ancient citadel, under the white Israeli flag curling in the desert breeze and brandishing its blue Star of David between broad blue bands like some Hasidic prayer shawl, modern Israeli soldiers take their oaths, vowing that "Masada shall not fall again."

Edmond Rothschild died in 1934. He did not live to see Partition by the United Nations in 1948, but he must have sensed that his dream was coming to fruition. It was to a Rothschild that the famous Balfour Declaration was written in 1917, declaring Great Britain's support for the establisment of Israel and paving the way for the country to be carved into modern history.

And, today, Masada stands.

9

Hard Work and Risk

Vanderbilt's Hundred Dollar Loan

The bright April sunshine smiled down on the boy in the half-plowed field. Though yet cool springtime, sweat glittered on his brow and his shirt was soaked through. He drew up on the reins, bringing the big mule to a stop, and wiped his forehead with an already dirty handkerchief. He stretched and rubbed his stiff back, gazing off longingly into the distance towards the water of New York harbor. The tall, blue-eyed boy couldn't see it, but he knew it was there, the periauger—a flat-bottomed, two-masted sailing scow, his ticket to freedom out of this accursed field.

A hundred dollars the man wanted; it might as well have been a million. His farm family didn't have that kind of money to throw around, and who would lend that much to a seventeen year old kid?

He glanced up at the sun again, nearly overhead. The shadow of an idea had been forming in his mind, as family legend tells it, and he began to gather his courage about him to plunge ahead.

Running his hand through his blond hair, Cornelius Vanderbilt set his jaw and determinedly guided the mule to the rail fence. He unhitched the traces, laying the plow over on its side and leading the thirsty animal to the watering trough for a drink. Impatient now, he watched the mule slurp long drafts of water, slaking his morning's thirst.

Hurriedly tying the animal in the shade, young Cornelius raced to the house. If he hurried, he could get there before his father came in from the field for lunch.

Young Vanderbilt scudded to a halt at the well, rapidly pumping it up and down. No sense trying to talk to his mother before washing up; she'd just send him back to do it anyway. It took the water a long time before it started to flow. How come it always took so long when he was in a hurry? The boy reached for the cup of water always left beside the well and poured it down the top of the pipe, priming the pump. Finally, cool water began to gush from the spout and he ducked his head under, washing the morning's grime and sweat from his hands and head.

Still dripping, Cornelius raced for the porch. The boy must have been very nervous. In those days, it was not only custom, but law, that required a son to work for his father until he reached twenty-one. Here he was, not even eighteen and already he was trying to get away from the back-breaking work of the farm.

His mother greeted him with a smile, possibly

stirring a pot of vegetable soup in preparation for the family's noon-day meal.

Haltingly, hesitantly, the boy poured out his hopes and dreams for the future to his mother. He had seen a wonderful sailing barge, Cornelius told her, it would be perfect for hauling vegetables. He could make enough money this summer to pay her back and earn more money to boot. Please. It wasn't as though he were asking her to *give* him the money, all he wanted was a loan.

Time must have hung very heavy that day in the Vanderbilt kitchen while the boy's mother considered. Finally, she looked at him, sternly, but with a trace of loving humor. Okay, she'd make a bargain with him. Yes, she would advance him the $100, but only if he plowed, harrowed, and planted the eight-acre corn field before his next birthday. But properly, you understand. No sense a-doin' something if you don't do it well.

Young Vanderbilt's face must have shown his joy, then consternation, almost all in the same instant. By his next birthday? Why, that was less than one month away. How could he ever get all that done in one month by himself?

By himself? His eyes narrowed thoughtfully. Here was the hope, the money; the barge was his, if he could work hard enough, fast enough. How badly did he want it?

Cornelius must have laughed out loud as his long legs carried him out the door and across the field to his neighbor's house. By himself, indeed. He'd just get some help.

The young man spent the next intense hours talking to his friends. Help me, he begged, and

135

I'll give you all the sailing rides you want. His friends listened with willing ears. It was a deal.

The next month was hectic, up early and working till there was no trace of light left to see the furrows. Cornelius found himself asleep almost before his head hit the pillow, only to rush from bed again at the first sound of cockcrow.

By his birthday, it was all done. The cornfield was plowed, harrowed until no more hard clods were left, and carefully planted in neat, even rows. He stood before his mother, eighteen years old, and ready to receive her part of the bargain.

The hundred dollars in hand, Cornelius Vanderbilt raced to the harbor to buy his barge. He was to say in later years that never, with all the money he had made, did he feel the satisfaction that he felt that wonderful morning when he stepped onto his own boat, "hoisted my own sail, and put my own hand on my own tiller."

All that long summer, Cornelius hauled produce from the farm to the city markets, and ferried folks from one side of the river to the other. It was said of him that people could set their watches by the promptness with which the young man arrived and departed. By the end of the summer, not only had he repaid his mother her $100, but he also owned three barges! The young man was on his way.

Hard work meant nothing to this man of vision. During the War of 1812, he shipped supplies to military posts, often working twenty-four to thirty-six hours without sleep. But, by the end of the war, he had earned enough to purchase a schooner.

In the next eleven years, Cornelius Vanderbilt made over ten million dollars. And it was then, and only then, that he sold out his fleet of ships and went into railroading, thereby to make his *real* fortune!

Men of millions and vision have one thing in common . . . courage to take enormous risks. When other men may hesitate, these men have seen a possibility and stepped ahead on faith, then worked to see that faith justified and their dreams come true.

At the end of World War II when governments were mothballing ships from war navies, Aristotle Onassis and Stavros Niarchos envisioned a world commerce starving for goods-carrying ships. Acting on faith, each man bought as many as he was able, sacrificing everything, building enormous fleets and, eventually, incredible fortunes.

Sometimes courage comes at moments when, acting on faith, a man is so heavily committed that there is nothing to do *but* forge ahead. In 1928, in the midst of building Rockefeller Center, one of the most ambitious building projects of modern times, the nation's economy crashed, the Depression was on its way. No one had any more money to pour into the project; tenants confirmed for the Center, such as the Metropolitan Opera, pulled out, leaving what looked like a vast unfinished white elephant sitting squarely on the hands of John D. Rockefeller, Jr.

What options were open to him? Would he quit, leaving a partially completed shell already having cost millions of dollars? How could he finance the completion with no prospective tenants? The situation looked grim at best.

But Rockefeller, discussing his decision later, modestly explained his reasoning. Sometimes, he said, people find themselves in a position where there is really only one option available to them. They may be scared and want to run away, but where does one run to? And, so, finally, you go ahead and do the only thing you can do, plunge ahead and finish it, and other people call it courage. Rockefeller would go ahead with the building, drawing on his own resources and on his immense faith in his nation's recuperative powers. Today, of course, Rockefeller Center includes seventeen large buildings, including the Metropolitan Opera and Radio City Music Hall, spread over fifteen acres in the center of New York City.

William F. Buckley, father of our current breed of conservative Buckley's, began building his fortune in the rowdy little border town of Washington de los Brazos, Texas. A man of considerable courage, Buckley emphasized his will by walking around gunless in a town where virtually every man daily strapped on a sidearm.

Buckley began to acquire oil leases, first in Texas and then across the border in Mexico. Facts of the time required the payment of bribes to Mexican officials. All the big oil barons had been forced to grease the palms of bureaucrats from the bottom up. But not Will Buckley. It was a matter of principle, he said, and, to Will Buckley, *nothing* came before principle. *Nothing*.

Despite his obstinence and the disapproval of the Mexican government, Buckley turned up with more and more choice oil leases. His name became a cuss word in the offices of certain Mexican officials. He was setting a bad example for others. If this was allowed to continue, everybody might refuse to pay the bribes. The word went out; get him.

Soon Will Buckley became aware of the presence of one Monty Michael and the boys, a gang with a Texas-size reputation as killers. His every footstep was dogged by the shadowy ne'er-do-wells.

Will Buckley handled the problem in his characteristic straight-forward manner. One evening, while on his way to a restaurant with friends, Will doubled back and confronted Monty. "Boys," he is reported to have told him, "I'm gonna go down here to get something to eat. Why don't you all run get yourself a bite to eat?"

The bad man was astonished. What was *wrong* with this dude? He began to stutter. "But don't you *know*....? If I can't scare you outta Mexico, then I've got orders to *kill* you!"

In this larger than life saga, Buckley is said to have smiled and told them they'd have about an hour before he would be ready to leave.

Each succeeding day became more frustrating for Monty and the boys. Once, while working in his warm office late at night, the outlaws shivered outside in the cold. Buckley sent out for coffee and sandwiches to keep them warm. The men did not understand this incredible man of Christian charity. Nothing in their mean and petty lives had taught them how to deal with these kinds of actions.

Finally, one night, Michael and the gang burst into Buckley's room, clearly at the end of their ropes. It was inconceivable that they should continue stalking the great man. They'd rather work *for* Mr. Buckley.

Why, they would go across to the cantina right now, sir. The men who hired them were there and the Michael gang would just prove their loyalty. They would kill these evil men who wanted Buckley dead.

Horrified, Will Buckley's mouth must have dropped full open. Here was a style of life *he* did not understand; such actions were not only uncharacteristic of him, but inconceivable in principle. "No!" he shook his head vehemently. "You boys can't do that!"

The outlaws were more confused than ever. Here was a man who was under sentence of violent death, yet he ever showed them kindness. Yet when they offered to turn and rend the attackers, he refused. They could not understand such a man. The outlaw band turned and walked out of Will Buckley's office, and out of his life forever.

But his trials with the Mexican government were not over. Pressure to pay the expected bribes became heavier and heavier; Buckley became persona non grata below the border. He was finally officially banished from the country, and over a million dollars in oil leases were confiscated by the government.

"I could have paid the bribes," he shrugged later, "but it was against principles." This was a lesson he deeply ingrained in all his children as well. If there is a choice between money and principles, he avowed, a man's principles *must* come first. *Always.*

Penniless now, but unabashed, William F. Buckley began working anew and before his death, he would amass a fortune of over 110 million dollars.

In a day when more yachts and homes and fine blooded horses were bought than could ever possibly be used, Cornelius Vanderbilt II, son of old Commodore Vanderbilt, stood alone as a man whose ideas of money usage grew in another vein. Not that he lived in poverty, not at all but it has been estimated that he gave away for charitable purposes from one-fourth to one-half his yearly income. Chauncey DePew, one of Vanderbilt's best friends, once noted that the great man attended services at his Episcopal church every single day and that every problem or opportunity brought to him must first be examined in light of whether or not it was right or wrong. No gray area for this Vanderbilt; his puritan upbringing considered everything in stark black or white. DePew went on to say of him, that once Vanderbilt was satisfied as to the moral correctness of his path, "no difficulties, no dangers, no obstacles deter him."

Each time a new employee began work for J. P. Morgan, the great man would come into the office during the orientation period. Stretching his hand as far over his head as it would go, he would instruct, "We do business up here," and those incredible ice blue eyes would glitter as he dropped his hand to the floor and continued, "not down here."

In every act of business in your life, first determine your dreams, as large and full as you can imagine them, then make absolutely certain your principles come first. Then, risking all, and, as the Biblical King David said in the Old Testament just before he died, "Be of good courage, and *do it.*